BEAT THE ODDS

The Exlusive Hotelier's Guide: Upsell Yourself and Succeed in a High Occupancy Job Market

MONA ALHEBSI

First published in 2018
Copyright © 2018 Mona Alhebsi

ISBN
Print: 978-0-6483402-4-9
Ebook: 978-0-6483402-5-6

All rights reserved. No part of this book may be reproduced, stored in a retrieval system, or transmitted by any means (electronic mechanical, photocopying, recording, or otherwise) without written permission from the author.

Because of the dynamic nature of the internet, any web addresses or links contained in this book my have changed since publication and my no longer be valid. The information in this book is based on the authors' experiences and opinions, the views expressed in this book are solely those of the author and do not necessarily reflect the views of the publisher, and the publisher herby disclaims any responsibility for them.

The author of this book does not dispense any form of medical advice, legal, financial or technical advice either directly or indirectly. The intent of the author is only to offer information of general nature to help you in your quest for personal development and/or self-help, in the event you use any of the information in this book the author and the publisher assume no responsibility for your actions. If any form of expert assistance is required, the services of a competent professional should be sought.

Publishing information

Publishing, design and production facilitated by Passionpreneur Publishing
www.PassionpreneurPublishing.com

Content developed using the services of the Ultimate 48 Hour Author
www.48HourAuthor.me

Tel: 1 300 664 006
Diamond Creek
Melbourne, Victoria
Australia 3089

Testimonials

"Mona AlHebsi is a gifted individual to work in the hospitality industry, especially in the Human Resources area because she understands the needs of the employees and the organization. She is one of the first UAE Nationals to start working in the hospitality industry and many people would love to read her hospitality experience, emphasizing the challenges she has encountered and how she has overcome them."

~ **Ibrahim Yaqoot**
Executive Director Corporate Support for
Dubai Department of Tourism and Commerce Marketing

"Hotelier and award-winning HR professional Mona AlHebsi wrote 'Beat the Odds' to share with others the winning ingredients of being a successful leader in the hospitality industry and how to overcome cultural differences, gender perceptions and increasing competition in the job market. Read this book and learn from one of the best."

~ **Judy Hou**
Managing Director for The Emirates Academy
for Hospitality Management

"With Beat the Odds, Mona AlHebsi will trigger the readers to consider working in an industry that at times is not as highly regarded as others and henceforth, dispel all the baseless myths about the nature of work in hotels. No one else can explain this as well as Mona, being herself immersed in the hospitality industry from a young age and considered a credible HR Leader for her peers and an admirable role model for Emiratis."

~ Caroline Stevens
Chief People Officer for Minor Hotels

"Mona helps you create a present and a future, overflowing with possibilities. Reading Beat the Odds is like having a private coaching session to take your life to the next level. It's compelling, thought-provoking, inspiring and uplifting all at once. This book is packed full of fascinating insights and fresh ideas and is an ideal addition to the bookshelf of any hospitality professional. It is an essential reading for anyone interested in hospitality and the importance of the industry to the economy of the 21st century."

~ Assia Riccio
Founder of Evolvin' Women

"I have known Mona for a few years now and she is a very authentic and motivated person. She has a strong background in HR with luxury hotels and has won many awards within the hospitality industry. Given her strong HR background and experience in the industry, Mona's book is highly recommended, and a must read."

~ Raj Bhatt
Chief Executive Officer & Director for Hozpitality.com

"You can't help but smile broadly whenever you meet Mona. Her love of the hospitality industry literally shines through in every interaction. She is a role model, whose passion for sharing has resulted in an inspirational book, packed with guidance on how to take ownership to create a meaningful career."

~ Hazel Jackson
Chief Executive Officer for Biz Group

"Mona truly has beaten the odds! She managed to figure out a way to turn the challenges that she faced into opportunities to excel in her career in a highly competitive industry. If there is a roadmap to beat the odds in the hospitality industry, then she has it."

~Moustafa Hamwi
The Passionpreneur, International Award-Winning Author & Speaker

"Mona is a valuable member of our advisory council and inspired us to focus on what's important to develop a pragmatic hospitality curriculum. Overcoming peer pressure or negative energy is extremely difficult, yet, Mona has chosen a career within an industry which may not have initially been well-received. Her book is a real case study in perseverance and determination and all credit to Mona for pushing through and taking the time to tell her story and share her expertise."

~ Jeff Strachan
Director of Business Development for Dubai College of Tourism

"I've known Mona since she was completing her ICF coaching certification and worked on coaching her 1-2-1 after that. Mona is a dedicated, trustworthy, and humble person. She is someone who loves working closely with people and bringing out the best in them. Mona is the best person to write this book, being an excellent example for courage and resilience in her industry. Her book will inspire you to think differently about your career."

~ Kevin Craig
*Executive Leadership Coach and Entrepreneur
& Author of Polar Bears and Penguins*

"Mona is a growth driven individual with high emotional intelligence and a firm belief that every individual has a spark and potential to always do better and more. I would definitely recommend reading Mona's book as here you would see real life experiences, challenges faced and ways to overcome them…in brief… Words of Wisdom that will inspire you to do things that matter and add meaning to your life."

~Dinesh Chaudhari
Associate Director of Learning & Development for Jumeirah Beach Hotel

"Mona is a sincere and committed professional. She works very hard to make a positive impact on the minds of people she interacts with. Mona is a great coach and I admire the way she has worked her way up to be what she has always dreamt to be. I am sure her book will be very valuable to anyone who wishes to climb the ladder and make it happen."

~ DR. R. L. Bhatia
Founder of World HRD Congress, World CSR Congress & Author of School Organisation and Management

Dedication

To my almighty God, who blessed me so much and guided me in every step of my life, thank you for enlightening me and utilizing me to serve my fellow human beings in every possible way I can.

★★★★★★★

To the marvelous Mona! Congratulations sweetheart; you have done it! You are finally a published author. All that endless work on weekends and evenings have proved worthy of effort and here you are spreading your message and checking another item off your dream list.

★★★★★★★

To my loving family, the essence of my being and a deeply rooted value in me, I'm very grateful to have each one of you in my life. Keep nurturing me with your love and encouragement to stay courageous and blossom.

★★★★★★★

To my adorable life partner who loved me unconditionally and supported me through the ups and downs, this work wouldn't have been possible without your companionship and patience.

★★★★★★★

To all those wonderful people who believed in me, cheered me up and showed camaraderie when I needed them, thank you from the heart as people like you make this world a great place to be in.

★★★★★★★

And lastly, to all veteran hotel professionals who put tremendous efforts day in and day out to serve others, take some time for yourself to read this book and implement the concepts discussed in it to take your hotel career to new heights.

★★★★★★★

Contents

Foreword **11**

Preface **15**

Chapter 1
Beat The Odds **21**

Chapter 2
Trust Your Intuition **45**

Chapter 3
Design Your Future **63**

Chapter 4
Celebrate Your Mistakes **83**

Chapter 5
Boost Your Credibility **99**

Chapter 6
Surprise Your Employer **117**

Chapter 7
Shout Your Success **139**

Chapter 8
Leverage Social Media **159**

Chapter 9
Expand Your Network **175**

Chapter 10
Snatch The Spotlight **197**

Chapter 11
Dare To Disagree **219**

Chapter 12
Pay It Forward **237**

About The Author **257**

Reading Recommendations **259**

Foreword

I first came to the UAE as a junior hotel executive in 1978. Now after 45 years, 30 of them in Dubai, I am delighted to have the opportunity to write the foreword for Mona AlHebsi's first book.

The UAE has always been a shining beacon of enlightenment in the Arab world. This is thanks to the current leadership of the UAE led by the President, H.H. Sheikh Khalifa bin Zayed Al Nahyan; the Vice President and Prime Minister, H. H. Sheikh Mohammed bin Rashid Al Maktoum, and H. H. Sheikh Mohammed bin Zayed Al Nahyan, the Crown Prince of Abu Dhabi and Deputy Supreme Commander of the UAE Armed Forces.

The founding fathers of the nation, the late H. H. Sheikh Zayed bin Sultan Al Nahyan, and the late H.H. Sheikh Rashid bin Saeed Al Maktoum established the conditions that encouraged the commitment to education for all Emiratis both male and female. The results of this visionary approach are obvious today with Emiratis leading in business and government at all levels.

Mona AlHebsi is a great example of how women of the UAE can achieve their potential by breaking taboos and fully participating in the incredible success of the UAE. There are nine female ministers in the cabinet of the Prime Minister, H. H. Sheikh Mohammed bin Rashid Al Maktoum including Her Excellency Reem Al Hashimi who is also the CEO for the Dubai World Expo 2020.

As the first CEO of the Jumeirah Hotel Group, I have always been proud of the hotel industry's support for women in the workplace. Mona's ground-breaking entry and participation in the industry is indeed inspiring. She has demonstrated to her fellow UAE nationals, males and females, that opportunities abound in Travel, Tourism and Hospitality within the UAE and globally. Thanks to ambitious women like Mona, Jumeirah Hotel Group employs over 300 UAE nationals in different business functions.

Travel and Tourism now accounts for 10% of global GDP and provides almost 300 million jobs worldwide. It is estimated that the contribution of the industry to Dubai's economy is as high as 25%. Mona made the right decision to beat the odds and venture into a field that may have not been quite favorable initially, her decision though, gave her the edge to be among those Emiratis who are the pioneers in hospitality and enabled her to set a successful example for other UAE Nationals who aspire to be part of the industry.

But, do not read this book just because Mona is a UAE National female; read it for the wealth of knowledge and advice that is so eloquently shared, for the skills and insights she has gained through her experience with leading hotels like Burj Al Arab, Hyatt Hotels, Jumeirah Creekside Hotel and Jumeirah Zabeel Saray.

I wish Mona continuing success in her chosen career. We are fortunate to have her!

Gerald Lawless
Chairman
The World Travel & Tourism Council,
2016 – 2018

Preface

1. Who is this book for?

'Beat the Odds' is my humble gift to all hoteliers who work very hard to deliver exceptional services and exhilarating experiences to internal and external guests day in and day out. It's a message to my industry peers; I applaud the great work they do for other people every day but would also like to remind them not to neglect their own selves either.

This is a practical, easy to follow guidebook wherein I have consolidated over 13 years of experience, lessons learned in my career and what I have done in different scenarios to achieve great success despite all the challenges I faced in the process. As I interact with more people during my working hours or any other professional setting, I can strongly see the need for such a book, with principles for hoteliers to practice, and reap long-term benefits for themselves and their organizations.

This book will give you access to tried and tested methods that you can follow to achieve great career success. Looking at the packed schedules and shifts of people working in the hotel industry, I have put together something which is to the point and effective in building a successful career. I am hopeful that this book will be beneficial for people who are too busy to figure things out for themselves.

'Beat the Odds' is not necessarily a "Secret Mantra" or a "Shortcut" that will grant you success overnight with minimum efforts; on the contrary, it's an eye-opening guidebook to what possibilities exist for you in this industry, if you choose to remove your blinkers and look at the bigger picture of your life, rather than spending your entire career being preoccupied with the smaller details.

2. Why did I write this book?

Reflecting on my life journey so far, it has always fascinated me how I've reached this point in my career regardless of all the obstacles and hurdles I faced along the way. Being in this path was completely my own choice with minimal support from those surrounding me at that time. Therefore, I needed to develop sufficient mental and emotional stamina in order to face whatever came my way.

At a certain stage in my early career, especially being a UAE National woman in an unconventional field i.e. hospitality, I had always wished for a blueprint or some set of guidelines that I could follow to achieve success sooner in my career. Unfortunately, I had to go through a series of trial and error exercises along the way to figure out what works and what doesn't. The good news is, it doesn't have to be the same for you. If you read, understand, and apply the principles discussed in this book, you can be well on your way to becoming the next star in the industry.

I wrote 'Beat the Odds' to highlight the importance of staying unique and how it will distinguish you from others in the industry. You can also choose to be ordinary like everyone else; however, that will not take you any further in your career or life. In order to stay unique, you need to be strong, well intended and constantly support your intentions with the right actions.

Over the years, I've realized that our intentions play a big role in shaping our future. They will dictate our means which in turn will determine our end results. Especially when working in a people centric industry like hospitality, having honest intentions and using ethical means in all your endeavors will always get you to your desired destination, even if sometimes it takes a long time to reach your goal. On occasions, you will even end up with a far better destiny than what you had envisioned for yourself, just because of your good intentions.

Following good intentions, you must focus on taking action in the right direction and delivering your best work every single day of your career. You will see further in this book that I've shared ideas and practices from my own life that helped me accelerate my journey to career success. Of course, I could have done it sooner if I had discovered these methods earlier. Now it's your turn; you can surely achieve the same outcome for your career if you choose to understand and apply the principles mentioned in this book.

3. How you can use this book?

Most parts of this book tackle mindset and behavioural changes that will help you as a professional hotelier to achieve optimum results for your career in the hospitality industry. This is based on my own life experiences and I've often supplemented the principles I've discussed in this book with life stories and examples to help you grasp the message. There are twelve chapters in the book, the first chapter examines some key aspects of my life and the factors that have contributed to shaping my personality. Sharing personal details of my life with my audience is quite important for me, not only to help readers realize that we all go through challenges in life, but also to reiterate that our responses to those challenges are what determines our life results.

The remaining eleven chapters in the book are dedicated to showcase a single success principle each. These principles are laid out in an easy to follow manner while tackling the benefits, the objections and the practical actions that the readers need to take in order to gain maximum benefits of each of the eleven principles in their career life.

I highly encourage you to read the book and do the exercises at the end of every chapter to get started with your journey towards career success. Once you have finished reading the book, you need to keep it as a quick reference and consult with it as often as possible to ensure that you remain on track.

You can also contact the author with any queries or feedback about the book using the contact details specified in the "About the Author" section of this book.

4. What inspired me to put it out there?

I was moved by the endless queries and encouragement notes that I have been receiving from people who know me either personally or professionally, commending my courage in beating the odds and the impact this has had on them. Some people are close relatives; others have been my colleagues for a good period of time and seen my work, and the rest are in my professional network. Especially lately, there have been several occasions when people asked me the common question "How did you do it?" or "What should I do to take my career to the next level?" This made me see the need for sharing my experience so that other people can relate to and benefit from it. Not only that, I've also tried to organize all these ideas in a methodical and easy to follow manner so that people who read this can implement what they learn instantly.

I therefore, invite you to take this enlightening journey and allow the "Star Hotelier" in you to shine, as I believe that you are capable of much more and you always deserve to be the best…

With all my Love and Respect,

Mona Abdulla AlHebsi

1
Beat The Odds

"Two roads diverged in a wood, and I took the one less travelled by. And that has made all the difference!"
~Robert Frost

I have dedicated the first chapter of this book to talk about significant life events and people who made an impact in my world. In the next few pages, you will discover various aspects of my life that have formed my personality and shaped my mindset.

The past is an integral part of our lives and we need to learn from it and use our past experiences as stepping stones to create a brighter present and future. Writing is a powerful tool, it provides us with an opportunity to reflect and rewrite our life story, so that pain becomes meaningful and promotes growth and transformation. As Fabian Linden said: "*It is useful occasionally to look at the past to gain a perspective on the present.*"

As you read through this section, you will be able to better relate to me as a person and understand my challenges, motives and aspirations. I'm also confident that you will connect emotionally and see something in it for yourself.

Get to Know Me...

I'm known as "Mona Abdulla AlHebsi" in terms of my worldly name. I'm a hotelier by profession and people person and writer by passion. I'm an Emirati by nationality and a female by gender. I'm an elder sister to my 7 siblings and the eldest child of my parents. Beyond all this, I'm a beautiful spirit from God who has inherited his attributes like my other human brothers and sisters. I don't claim to be better than anyone; every one of us is the same, the difference is in our results. I'm aware that I'm a unique and exclusive creature of God with high intelligence and deep intellect.

Baby Mona

I love life and want to make the most out of it as I know I'll only live once. Therefore, I strongly believe that it's an absolute waste to tiptoe through this life

During My MBA Graduation 2012

hoping to make it safely to death. What a dumb game to live like that!!! I want to experience and experiment with everything this life has to offer, I want to live a full life and inspire people around me to do the same. Like all of you, I have my own fears and insecurities, however, I trust that I have a God who is always there to protect and guide me. I also know that I'm courageous enough to move past those negative inclinations and voices and create the life I long for!

My Leading Source of Inspiration...

It's strange to say so, but, I seem to be very inspired by those people who "don't have", "can't be" or "won't do", whether those people are in my immediate circle or far away. Here, I am referring to those people who always have ready excuses why they don't have "motivation" or can't be "successful" or won't do the necessary work to get where they want to be in life. I however, always like to challenge the status quo and bring hope and positive change to the world. One thing I know from my life experiences so far is that if there is a will, there is a way. I don't believe in excuses. I have very high standards in life and know that nothing is impossible. I struggle to work with people who don't have a purpose and can't excel in something. I accept everyone around me as all of us here are going through our own life journey and are constantly learning and evolving at a conscious level. I also strive to help those around me who need guidance and direction to get closer to their goals. I just don't like to see people accepting to be average and not learning from their mistakes to improve the quality of their lives. I'm inspired by all those people who have ready excuses for why they are doing or not doing something. I enjoy accepting those challenges that the majority say are "impossible" or "not doable" and turning them into realities.

The Impact of Women in My Life...

The women who played a big role in shaping my personality are "My Mother" and then "My Sisters" and I'll tell you why.

With My Mother During Global HRD Summit 2016 in Mumbai

My mother is a simple woman whose parents didn't allow her to complete her education. She was the only girl in her family and she had only one brother. Still, her parents got her married at a very young age and then sent her abroad with her husband, where she struggled a lot in life. According to her, her family didn't back her in the most critical periods of her life. All my childhood, and even to this day, she has been telling me all sorts of stories on how she could have lived a good life if she had been better educated. Another thing, because she comes from a somewhat constrained environment, she didn't have the luxury to make key life decisions, like the right to be educated and to get married to the person of her choice, so she chose to become the victim of circumstances. She is always blaming everyone else except herself. She blames her family, the society, the circumstances, etc. for her current conditions. This has developed my personality in big way. I've always seen my mother as someone with a tendency to conform, to fit in, in order to be accepted, which hasn't got her very far in life. Therefore, I wanted to be responsible for creating my own dream life myself. Regardless of the background I come from and the limitations that were imposed on me as a child; I will always appreciate my mother's many sacrifices for me and my siblings but will never adopt the same submissive approach as her to lead my own life. I also cannot forget how my mother has supported my desire for education and argued with my father to allow me to go to school. I worked very hard since my early

With My Mother and Brother Faisal

years in life and I was always exceptional and the best throughout the various stages of my education and career. I want to lead my life in a totally different way because I'm educated, and I know better.

I'm doing this for myself first, for my mother to be proud of me, but also being an elder sister, I want to be a source of inspiration to my four younger sisters and want them to know that "they also can do it" and live the life they deserve. I'm proud to say that each one of them is doing very well in her respective field. I'm inspired by all those women who have been told that they are less and don't have choices. I must take courageous steps in life no matter how scary they may appear in the beginning. We either turn things to our advantage or let life turn us in all different directions claiming that we are powerless. I reject being powerless. I refuse to be the product of circumstances. I dismiss any idea, belief or tradition that doesn't serve me and disgraces God.

Old Photo with My Four Sisters

My Learnings from My Parents...

I believe my parents did their best with the knowledge and

experience they had at that time to raise me and my siblings and provide us with good living conditions. I still remember how my mother worked very hard at home to raise 8 children alone without a maid. Being the eldest, I started helping her out with home chores at a very young age. I always remember being the eldest and the most responsible and don't really remember much other childhood details like other kids. I also remember my father being a very simple person (also the eldest in his family). He also was not educated and used to work hard and do different shifts to provide a living for us. So, I guess, I've willingly embraced being responsible, having a passion for service and caring for others, like my parents and I believe these characteristics represent a big part of my personality. Family is one of my core values, so I always like to go back to my hometown Ras Al Khaimah during weekends and holidays to spend time with my family.

My Parents in Dubai Metro

On the other hand, some early childhood messages (or what I call conditioning) have been causing me lots of pain and hindering my progress; values like we must obey elders or seniors, no matter what they say or do, we must put others first before ourselves, we must conform to traditions and society expectations etc. in addition to various other misconstrued things that I was made to believe about my religion.

As I learnt, researched and evolved, I discovered that most of these things have confused and inhibited me more than serving me to reach my goals. It took me a good number of years to say no to most of these things, and I'm still figuring out some more. Of course, it made some people unhappy with me and I had to go through some challenging periods in my life because I chose to

Winning the 100 Most Influential Global HR Professionals Award 2017 in Mumbai

act differently and not conform. I chose to consult with the "real Mona" not the "conditioned Mona" in my key life matters. Now I'm grateful that I'm doing so because I'm getting great results and progress in my life. God gave us brains to think and reason and, in my opinion, if we decide to choose conditioning over our thinking abilities then we are the only ones to blame.

My Take on Culture and Traditions...

As I mentioned above, there was a lot of confusion created in my early life because I was told that certain things were core parts of our religion that we need to follow without questioning. This happened at home, at school by some teachers who were themselves confused or the media (which you may know by now is mostly propaganda). As the verse in the Holy Quran says: "Oh you, who believe, whichever piece of information you receive, check it out first" 49.6, urging us not to believe everything we hear and to check the source of information properly first. This is what I strive to follow ever since I understood this verse and its implications. I realized that in order to know the religion better, we need to check the Holy Scriptures not the people's understanding of what is in the scriptures. I also learnt that sometimes, people try to impose what they want under the name of religion, so, many traditional sayings and practices for example don't make sense, but people still follow them because they were told it's part of the religion and they just followed it without thinking. Then they complain, why are we not getting the results we want even though we follow the "religion," seriously?! Understanding these fine lines of life made me see things with better clarity and learn how to respond when someone tries to interfere or attempt to convince me to do things their way.

My culture is rich with some great traditions like hospitality, being brave, generosity, respect and having a flair for words and wisdom. I'm proud to have those positive elements in my personality. I just refuse any other characteristic that doesn't value the uniqueness of an individual and expect him/her to be a follower and not think for himself/herself. Freedom is my core value, so I'm against anything and everything that rips people away from their birthright freedom of choice, expression, and living the life they see for themselves. I don't see how making one person's life miserable can make the society grow and prosper. It's very contradictory.

My Father with Hebsi Tribe During A Traditional Wedding in RAK

I want to bypass fake customs that don't benefit humanity and don't bring value to make them live their life with more dignity and joy. For instance, a practice that urges individuals to just be blind followers and dismiss their unique contributions and expressions is definitely not very impactful. I don't care if someone likes me or not, I will always keep going through life focusing on my greater purpose. One thing I know for sure, I can become and achieve whatever I want, so I'll do just that!

My Views on Conformity and Blending In...

Anyone who knows me very well will tell you that my whole life has been a continuous series of "beating the odds" and being the "exception to the rules" surrounding me. As I continue to evolve and learn more about myself and life, I realize that all outstanding people who left a mark in history have done exactly the same and therefore

With My Brother Mohammad and Niece

they are being remembered as great examples in their respective fields. They definitely faced a lot of resistance and sarcasm from people around them, but they persisted because they could see what others were not able to see at that point. I personally don't know of any successful personality who only followed mainstream beliefs and then became a celebrity or someone of immense authority.

In essence, being true to ourselves means to honor our capacity to use our brains and know it's not sinful to activate our abilities to think, make judgments and choose what's right for us. More than often, we are encouraged throughout the various stages of our life whether by parents, society, educational institutions or media to be followers and deactivate our brains. As a result, we become "conditioned" beings who copy and paste behaviors around us without thinking whether these behaviors will serve us or not. God created each of us with our own life purpose to be unique,

The First Group of Emiratis in Jumeirah with CEO Gerald Lawless in 2005

nonetheless, we strive to follow others and shy away from exhibiting our distinctiveness, even if we have to pay a huge price as a result of this choice. This in itself shows how dangerous the impact of conditioning can be on human minds; that they won't mind rejecting clear life related facts in order to fulfill the expectations of their conditioning.

These beliefs acted as one of my driving forces to join the world of hospitality at a time when this was not very common among my peers. Even nowadays, you will still hear people who criticize the idea of being a female and working in a hotel. It's just not being perceived favorably and may affect other areas in life like family approval and marriage. Besides, Emiratis have a strong preference for government jobs as it is considered more secure, family friendly because of the short hours and long holidays, and offers more pay and perks to locals. In the beginning, I always used to worry about my future and the fact that I would be less popular among my peers and society in general if I opt to work in a "hotel." Yet, there was a fierce innate drive that urged me to do my internship in Hilton in 2004, which was an important requirement to complete my degree program. I was supposed to complete a 2-month work placement and for reasons I didn't know at that point, it had to be a hotel. The response at home was not very welcoming initially; however, I managed to persuade my parents that this is what I desire to do. My female class fellows exclaimed at my decision and tried their best to convince me to change my mind and select a bank or a government department instead. The one person who encouraged me and cheered my decision at that time was my business professor who proudly told me: "Well done! You will be the one who will drive the change in this environment!" I was really motivated by his words and got excited about the idea to be "The Change Agent." Soon enough, I loved the royalty and the glamour I experienced during my time in Hilton. I also enjoyed the frequent interactions with new people that added to my learnings. Even today after more than 14 years since that first hotel experience, I still enjoy every bit of it and have learnt how to make it even more rewarding. I have realized after many years that I'm doing what represents me, in term of exclusivity, quality, service and uniqueness. I wouldn't have been as happy and successful if I'd have prioritized following others over my true calling. It's not easy to attempt to standout in a society that believes a woman's role is to merely sit at home and raise children. If you choose to listen to your heart and ignore everything else, you may risk the love and acceptance of your family, friends and society, at least temporarily. That's why, it's very important that every one of us must know our own guiding principles and core values to help identify our priorities in life. It's true that where some people may value harmony and others acceptance, some like me would be guided by being unique and more exclusive, and these elements mainly drive my key decisions in life. The point here is, once you find yourself, your worry about losing others will become secondary.

Dealing with Others' Expectations...

Since my life journey towards knowing the truth began, I'm always trying to do "what's right" not "what's common." I'm also aware that many people won't accept that because they are either conditioned not to think or because it goes against their personal agendas. In the beginning, any brave step I took brought a lot of resistance, however, interestingly, as I kept on doing more of the unconventional stuff, I noticed people went away from my path because they knew I was very determined and will do what I see right no matter what. Throughout my family or work life I faced a lot of scenarios when people expected me to be a follower and do what everyone else is doing (meaning to be just average).

One of my key strengths is "Significance." I hate to be in a place where my presence is equal to my absence. If I'm working for a certain company, then I'll make sure that I create moments and results that will be remembered by people around me long after I'm gone. And I know, this will happen only if I do things differently and not when I just fit in and do what others are already doing.

Winning Asian Women Leadership Awards 2015 in Dubai

I react in different ways, (cannot help it) especially when I see my key values being compromised. For example, when someone tries to control my freedom, or when I see people around going through life without a purpose or meaning; the wise and courageous Mona will rise all of a sudden and will take charge to bring things under control. I admit that when this happens, I leave people around in a state of astonishment, trying to figure out what just happened, and believe me it is fun to do that! In addition, I'm a very spiritual person and believe that things like faith and trust work big time and in occasions can turn things miraculously to your advantage if you stay focused and continue doing what you are supposed to do. I always turn to God when I'm lost or when I don't know what to do and he gives me the guidance I need. I keep my focus on acquiring knowledge and continuously learning new things to expand my horizons. Knowledge is power and the more you know the more powerful you are.

Other Peoples' Perceptions and Opinions…

The importance we place on other people's opinion of us will greatly depend on our current level of consciousness and wisdom. This will define our priorities and what to focus on. I personally choose to stay focused on my goals. Here I'm not trying to sound idealistic, as in some occasions it really matters what those close to me think about me and my actions. However, with time, I learnt that it's in my hand to allow other people's perception to control me or I can choose to shift my focus to what's more important in my life. So that I can deliver great results and thus change other people's perception of me and my work, even though it's not the driving factor for me.

As Stephen R. Covey mentions in his book "The 7 Habits of Highly Effective People", you get more done when you choose to shift your focus from the circle of concern, things you cannot change to circle of influence, things you can change and thus manage to get more control over your life.

During My Time with Grand Hyatt Dubai

Creating Inspiration from Life Events...

As the saying goes, successful people see the opportunity in every adversity and others see the adversity in every opportunity. I believe every life event has a positive message no matter how we choose to initially interpret it. Even the most unfortunate life scenarios turn into great blessings in the long run if we persist and practice patience. It's the way we think that determines our next course of action. That's why it's rightly said that life is about 10% of what happens to you and 90% how you choose to react to it. I'm no different to other people when it comes to challenges. I have my fair share of challenges and honestly, this is what keeps me going and has led me to my greatest breakthroughs so far. The moment I learnt to change my outlook towards various life challenges, it helped me a great deal and made me turn them into vehicles to get me closer to my goals.

Winning The Best Student Award During My Graduation In 2004 From HCT

Before anyone else, I'd like to assure myself that regardless of all the current circumstances that appear against me, I can still do it and reach where I want to be. The next step becomes figuring out the "how". Here comes the role of goal setting and breaking them down into small actionable steps to get myself there. It's a simple rule of life which once understood, can really take you to places you have never dreamt of. This, when followed constantly and with resilience, will get you from one success to another, and ultimately, it will make those around you take notice of the difference in your results and feel inspired. Any success story is mostly preceded by lots of failures, sacrifices and yet, continuous learning and a strong desire to succeed. Just remember to count even your smallest blessings during those difficult times; they will help you to slowly but surely pass through those periods and reach your most awaited destination.

Bringing My Personality into the Various Roles in My Life...

I learnt to be able to see myself beyond any roles I fulfil i.e. daughter, sister, employee, manager, etc. only a few years ago. All thanks to my continuous learning journey and specifically my coaching certification program and other personality assessment tools wherein I learnt more about myself and the impact I have on my surroundings. I learnt that there is a difference between just playing the role like everyone else and bringing my characteristics to these roles to fulfil them in a unique way. It's in the style I perform these roles that my core values and strengths become obvious to myself and others. To give an example, I generally have a futuristic outlook on things and by nature I'm someone who lives in the future. It always fascinates me to imagine how my relationship with my husband will look like after 5, 15 or 30 years of marriage. What life adventures will we have together? What will be our marriage lessons that we can pass on to our children, where will we be living? Where will I be in terms of career growth? If I choose to have my own business, what will it look like, etc. Then, I write the answers to these on a piece of paper and turn those into actionable goals, and figure out ways to turn them into reality. So, you can imagine that most of my discussions with the people I know would be about the possibilities for the future and how we can afford a better life for ourselves and our children rather than dwelling on past events.

In my professional life for instance, I'm very adamant that my team members continue learning and improving themselves, deliver their best work and collaborate as a team to transform something strong into something superb. I expect them to continuously challenge themselves and operate with the highest levels of conduct, because quality, learning and ethics are among my key values. This may initially make me a hard person to work for, but with time, my employees see the value they get for themselves and their careers by integrating these principles in their

With One of My Team Members at Work

daily work. Because of these values and the results my employees have been getting, I've developed a reputation for being a sought-after leader that young talent in my industry and field would like to work for. I regularly receive a considerable number of requests through email and social media from people who would love to be a part of my team or ask for coaching or guidance to learn how to develop their careers.

My Most Important Source of Wisdom...

My first source of wisdom is myself. I trust God has given each one of us all the knowledge we require to do what needs to be done. I believe we need to dig deep into ourselves to get to know us better and discover the treasures we have been gifted with. We are naturally creative, resourceful and whole and we have all the answers we need within ourselves. We further need to supplement this with a curiosity to know and follow through with continuous formal and informal learning.

We learnt through childhood conditioning to interpret life events through our sensory experiences and ignore our most powerful ally that is, our intuition or gut feeling. I personally trust that God is very kind and merciful and he wouldn't leave us to shuffle through this life alone without guidance. He has provided each one of us with an internal GPS system to help us navigate through various life roadmaps and find the easiest way to get us to our goals. It's our fault if we choose not to use this GPS; then we cannot blame God when we remain behind or take too long to reach our destination. There is no point in blaming

the car manufacturer if we choose not to use the provided GPS to guide us in our journey, so that we can reach our destination sooner and with less trouble.

Over time and with constant conditioning we are made to believe that only what we can sensibly see, hear, touch, taste and smell, in other words, senses that are controlled by our brain, are the only things to be trusted. We have automatically given these senses more control on the way we perceive the world around us. When it comes to making key decisions about our personal life, business or relationships, we tend to silence or ignore any gut feelings just because we don't know how to quantify these feelings and never learnt how to use and trust this great tool. Think about a time in your life when you had a very uncomfortable feeling about someone, but you still chose to ignore those feelings and trust that person. You must have regretted your decision sooner rather than later because this person was not trustworthy, but you had decided to believe what others told you about him/her over your own instincts. Ever since I connected with myself and learned to listen to my intuition more than my brain's logical justifications, I started progressing forward in relatively all areas of my life. The intuition has the pure programming that God has installed in us when the soul was breathed into us and this is where we should go first to seek wisdom and guidance. In the next chapter, you will learn more about why it's a good idea to trust your intuition and how to go about it.

Suggested reading for this chapter:

If you've ever thought, "There must be more to life than this," The Art of Non-Conformity is for you. In this book, Author Chris Guillebeau defies common assumptions about life and work while arming you with the tools to live differently.

You'll discover how to live on your own terms by exploring creative self-employment, radical goal-setting, contrarian travel, and embracing life as a constant adventure.

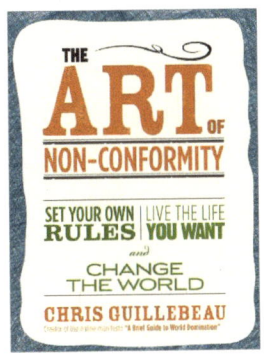

"Don't be ashamed of your story, it will inspire others."
~Tom Stoppard

2
Trust Your Intuition

"Always stand up for what you believe in… even if it means standing alone."
~ Kim Hanks

Gut Feeling or Intuition has always been called "The Highest Form of Intelligence" and the path to true happiness. God has given us several options to achieve our goals in life; some of us choose the simple ways and others pick the complicated ones. At the end of the day it's our choice, and we are the only ones to blame if we choose to ignore our internal compass and look for answers in places outside ourselves. Following are five benefits of trusting your intuition:

1. Develop deeper self-knowledge and inner connection…

Trusting your intuition gives you the opportunity to know yourself better. You will know your likes, dislikes, values, things you won't tolerate, etc. then act according to them.

In other words, you will have a solid ground or source on which you can base your life decisions at any given point and time. You will develop a better connection and trust with yourself when you learn to regularly understand and listen to your inner voice.

2. Make better decisions...

Self-trust allows you to make better quality decisions. The more decisions you bravely make based on your intuitive urges, the more skillful and experienced you will be in making the right decisions in various life scenarios. This is one of the key factors that distinguishes high performing leaders from others when it comes to combining both tangible i.e. visible and measurable data points like researches & statistics and non-tangible i.e. abstract inputs like hunches and feelings to make the right decisions. In fact, I'll go further and claim that statistics may at times deceive you, but, your intuition may not.

3. Increased happiness and reduced depression...

If you ignore your intuition, you will mostly regret it and vice versa. All the stories that I proudly tell others about my life were the recipes of trusting my intuition. I always have two options in any given scenario, the first is thinking like the common person, I get so terrified to take my next steps because this approach is usually guided by fear. The second option is to pause and ask myself: "What does Mona want?" Then do that, in those kinds of scenarios, I am guided by my inner wisdom. The proudest moments of my life are a result of being guided by "What does Mona want?" I did not care what others would think about me, I just did what I saw right. I still feel alive when I remember those stories; one of them is definitely my decision to enter the hospitality industry regardless of all resistance I faced from other people around me. Another example is the various decisions I make daily in my workplace despite all the hindrance I face initially, only to have it turn out to be the right things to do. That is what makes life happy and worth living. I encourage you to listen to your intuition to increase your happiness and minimize your regrets.

4. Hear the voice of caution and minimize risks...

Get used to the practice of taking your internal alarms seriously. I've read many stories of people who decided to ignore the caution signals that came from within about a boss, co-worker or a relative, which they then deeply regretted. If you ever have those uncomfortable feelings about something or someone, you have them for a reason. Learn to acknowledge those feelings, process them as a valuable source of information and dare to follow them. I promise you that you will be happier for doing that.

5. Be in charge and in control of your own life...

Who would be the best person to tell you what suits

you, what's good or what's bad for you? Who other than yourself, even though we have been conditioned to think otherwise? Most people go through life on autopilot because these are the very people who mostly ignore their hunches and do everything else for fake prestige or pleasing others, and this is very dangerous. They unwittingly harm themselves. If you want to be more in charge of your destiny, then trust your intuition and it will never let you fail.

★★★

Studies done at the Max Planck Institute amongst others have shown that intuitive decisions are reached faster and are subjectively 'better' than those landed on by purely rational means. Studies show that those who actively work on developing their intuition are capable of making better, faster, and more beneficial decisions.

Throughout my life and especially during my career in hospitality, I've always heard the expression "The Numbers Tell A Story" which encourages us to quantify and rationalize our decisions to ensure they will be accurate. Yes, I agree, the numbers may tell a story, but they definitely don't tell the full story! As humans, we need to learn how to trust our intuition as an important source of information to help us make accurate life decisions, especially the key ones. Here, I talk from my personal experience and I'm glad that I've followed my inner voice most of the time in my life because it proved to be right for me.

Data + Intuition = Better Decisions

Your intuition knows things that you don't. This is really a powerful tool that you cannot afford to ignore or not explore. It communicates with you through feelings. If you have a certain gut feeling, it's for a reason and it's right. If you follow it, you will win and if you choose to ignore it you will most probably regret the consequences and take longer to reach your goals. Recall most of the scenarios when you have decided to go against your gut feeling, you will notice a theme of regret, dissatisfaction and missing out. On the other hand, contemplate on those situations when you decided to listen to your instincts, you will remember feelings of pride, happiness, and fulfilment. Choose which one you want to experience frequently. The decision is yours!

Trusting your intuition is the right thing to do even though it may not be highly encouraged in society and corporate settings. Connecting with your intuition becomes even more important if you work in service-oriented industries like hospitality, due to the nature of work there and the need for regular interactions with people, whether they are co-workers, managers, guests, suppliers, or owners. Deep connection with own self and listening to your hunches will help you develop more meaningful relationships with others around you and proactively identify people and opportunities that will uplift or dispirit you in your career journey and make the right decisions about them accordingly.

There may be many questions running in your head about how viable is trusting your intuition and how much would it help you in your daily life. I'm including below three key objections I've heard from people when I encourage them to trust their intuitions, along with my responses:

O1 *What if people in my workplace call me "emotional" because I'm known to base my decisions mostly on gut feelings and not as much on rigorous data as is the practice in most corporate institutions?*

R1 Beware! Don't always take such comments negatively or as a sign of criticism. In fact, it may well be the total opposite. Today we live in a world where most people are disconnected from their own selves and consider emotions a sign of weakness. We are taught from a very young age to be more rational and less emotional. In my view, the most successful people among us are those who have the courage to show vulnerability and can connect easily with their own emotions which in turn help them make better life decisions. Intuitive feelings make us human and prevent us from becoming robots and machines that operate on fed data and programming alone. Such a comment could be either a commendable or envious testimony from a co-worker or manager who is indirectly telling you that you are more human than them and that they wish they were like you.

Nonetheless, if you regularly receive such comments in the workplace as an employee, you need to seek more fact based clarifications from the person who is providing the feedback. In case the feedback is genuine, start acting upon it to improve. On the other hand, it may well be that there is a clash between your internal values and the organizational values, or more likely, the values of the people you are working with. In that case, you need to decide what's more important to you and follow the same.

During A Sahaja Yoga Meditation Session Organized for Employees in The Hotel

Q2 *What if I continuously get judged and criticized about my decision-making style at work because it doesn't follow the traditional methodological approach of decision making?*

R2 Let's be practical here; you get to make it very simple for yourself and other people around you. In real world, people get judged and evaluated on their results and outcomes rather than their methodologies. Everything around us is rapidly changing and there are many occasions at work where immediate decision making is required. Especially when dealing with people, paying attention to your instincts about them will mostly pay off.

Your intuition is always accessible, truthful and provides you with a credible mean to make the right decisions. So, as long as your key performance results are achieved using the right approaches, it's less likely that someone will ask you to elaborately explain the steps you used to get there!

Q3 *What if I follow my intuition and then things don't work out as well as expected?*

R3 There are many elements to this question. First of all, trusting your intuition doesn't mean at all to talk loudly without thinking. One of the best things you can do when you are required to answer or make a decision is to pause for a while and notice your feelings as well as your thoughts. Learn to distinguish true intuition from impulsive egoic tendencies. Your ego will mostly be ridden by your fears and insecurities which usually doesn't have any base in reality. Your intuition though is the place where you get wisdom and guidance. In the beginning, if you are not much used to it, you may make a few mistakes, until you master your inner connection with yourself and know the difference between intuition and ego. Ego is mostly led by thoughts while intuition by feelings.

After tackling the main concerns people usually have about trusting intuition, let's learn how to develop a stronger relationship with our internal world and be more connected with our intuition through 3 simple practices:

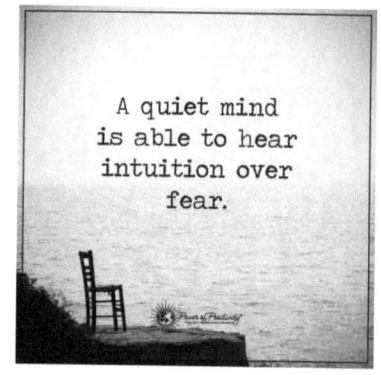

A quiet mind is able to hear intuition over fear.

1. Connect and befriend your intuition

Most people find "intuition" an abstract concept and that's why they don't understand it and avoid discussing it. In simple terms, intuition is a strong urge or drive that you get in different forms (mostly in the gut) to do or not do something. In order to strengthen your interpretation and trust in your intuition, you need to allocate dedicated periods to silence the noise in your head i.e. thoughts, disconnect from the outer world and only concentrate internally.

Calm App for Meditation

There are different ways in which you can do this. For example, one significant way is by being a more spiritual person. Whether you follow a certain religious ritual, recite some prayers, or do righteous deeds like charity and helping others, trust that all these practices will enhance your character and make you strong from the inside. Notice that the most effective people around you are also spiritual, regardless of the faith they follow. They make sure to indulge in some sort of prayers or good deeds that gives them benefits beyond their limited physical aspects and abilities. Another common way to deepen your connection with yourself is to do regular meditation. This helps you stand still, focus on your breath, and notice the kind of thoughts running in your head. This has proved a very useful technique for me, it gave me strength to carry on during some stressful moments of my life. I encourage you to be disciplined enough to meditate for at least 10 minutes every day if not more. Also, consistency is more important than time.

I've also recently heard about the power of silence and how some people practiced continuous silence for three days and more and got transformational results in their lives. In fact, during the last Leisure Show in Dubai, I was reading about top trends in wellness, spas, and travel in 2017, and silence was the number 3 emerging trend in

Credits: Thomas Smetena (THERME & SILENT SPA)
Christian Wöckinger HOTEL

the world. Also, I've read that the first completely "Silent Spa" has opened at Austria's Therme Laa Hotel and many more to follow in different parts of the world.

I was also surprised after reading about the benefits of silence to see that it's mentioned in the Holy Quran as an act of worship! When you are silent, you are more focused internally than externally and that enables you to receive inspirational messages from God that you cannot hear when you are always in action or surrounded by a lot of people and noise.

Last but not least, you also have to be aware of your feelings and understand them. Sense how you feel in moments of confusion and what your body is trying to communicate to you through feelings of comfort or discomfort. That's your clue on how to proceed forward. Spirituality, meditation, silence, and feelings are all tools to help you stay more connected to your inner voice and hear it more clearly, so learn to trust it as a valuable source of information.

Working in hospitality demands being very attentive and focused externally on other people to provide them with high-quality service. It doesn't give you much time to disconnect and concentrate on yourself. Just unplug to rejuvenate and recharge yourself. That will help you perform optimally, by making better decisions and comfortably enduring the long hours and demanding requirements of your job.

In my capacity as Head of HR in my organization, I facilitate most of the disciplinary discussions concerning major offenses with the suspected colleagues and their line managers. Over the past few years, and with consistent practice, I've developed a very strong sense of other people, I mean having the ability to know who is telling the truth and who is trying to flip the facts. I start getting my intuitive messages within a few minutes of talking to the person and observing his/her body language. These messages have turned out to be the right ones in around 95% of the cases. Of course, we follow company policies and procedures to discipline such employees, but it's never one size fits all. There were occasions when I would've got all the information necessary to dismiss an employee because of a gross misconduct. However, I had strong internal feelings of discomfort about that decision. In such cases, I purposely delay the disciplinary hearing to think over the case. I read the incident report and statements again. If necessary, I view the CCTV coverage and meet the people concerned myself, in addition to discussing the situation with the regional HR experts in the company to get insights. It's very challenging when you get to decide someone's destiny so it's necessary to do your due diligence. In majority of those cases, my first instincts were right. After taking my time to review things over and over or after getting more information I have found the missing links and thus managed to make the best decision for the employee concerned, as well as the company.

2. Notice your body and feelings when it comes to certain practices, behaviors, and situations.

As mentioned earlier, your feelings are a very valuable source of information. Don't ignore your feelings to please someone. The more you compromise, the more unfavorable scenarios you will end up being in. If you do compromise to please other people, they will get what they want, but you will be the one to suffer the consequences. The consequences can be personal like dealing with the fact that you've let yourself down or reputational like the image people will have about you, that you are someone who they can easily manipulate to get what they want from. Also observe what happens to your body when you come across certain situations or people. Do your hands become cold? Do you start sweating? Or do you get very strong sensations in your gut? Many research results suggest that feelings and intuition are based in the gut and that's why we call it "gut feeling", so we might as well pay more attention to what our bodies are trying to tell us.

3. Find out your core values and strengths as your intuition is closely aligned with them.

The earlier you learn this in your life, the clearer your path will become. The first step is to identify your core values. These represent your unique, individual essence and what you stand for. Your values drive your behaviors and provide you with a personal code of conduct. You rise when you honor your values and you suffer physically, mentally, and emotionally when you decide to repress them. I've personally discovered my core values during my coaching certification with CTI. Most people don't know their values and that's why they struggle to prioritize and know what's important to them in life. As a result, they focus on what society, culture and media promote and value, but still feel lost and unfulfilled.

Once you've identified your values, discover your strengths or "native geniuses". These are basically the things that you are naturally good at and you can also call them talents. I've started developing some basic idea about my strengths through observing the patterns in my life and noticing what elements of my personality usually get commended by those around me or get me maximum positive results in what I do. Further, I was introduced to the Gallup Clifton Strengths Finder Assessment and completed it. This is an amazing tool and helped me vividly understand my key strengths and thus I was able to connect all my previous success behaviors and effectiveness to the fact that I was intuitively utilizing my strengths and developing them into prevailing talents. This made me stand out and gave me the ability to highlight what I can do with excellence.

> "IT'S NOT HARD TO MAKE DECISIONS WHEN YOU KNOW WHAT YOUR VALUES ARE"
> – ROY DISNEY

Freedom is one of my core values. If you know me well, you may smile when you read this line but I'm not someone who likes to be restrained, whether it's at home, work, or other aspects of my life. You will see me making a lot of noise to do things the way I see right, and I rarely follow others or take instructions, especially if those instructions are not in line with my values and morals. In other words, since I know that freedom is one of my core values, it has helped me understand that my intuition will always urge me to align with this value. For example, I'll have very uncomfortable feelings in scenarios of micromanagement or when someone forgets to treat me like an individual adult and tries to dictate what I should do or shouldn't do. Conversely, I'll be at my best when I make my own decisions or guide my life in the way I see fit. I've actually met people who told me that they get overwhelmed when they have to decide for themselves, which shows we are all different and so are our values.

Self-Assurance is one of my dominant themes in the Clifton Strengths Finder Assessment. According to Clifton Assessment; people with strong 'Self-Assurance' are the ones who feel confident in their ability to manage their own lives. They possess an inner compass that gives them confidence that their decisions are right.

I can immediately see the connection between my value of freedom and my self-assurance strength and could recall the uncountable scenarios in my life when my intuition drove me to make unique decisions that were unheard of in those particular times, but later went on to be big inspirations and opened new doors to people around me. Of course one of them is my determination to choose a career in the hospitality industry. So, the next time whenever you encounter people at work who are trying to place you in confusing scenarios, stop and re-visit your core values and key strengths, then act in

accordance to them. You have no idea how fulfilled you will be and the outcome will eventually turn out to be the best one for you.

3 Actions you should take as a result of reading this chapter:

1. Undergo appropriate practices that you can adopt to hone your connection with yourself. Perhaps you need to try meditating for at least 21 days or choose to isolate yourself from other people in a quiet place and observe at least 3 days of complete silence. This will help you focus inward and learn to listen to your internal messages. I use an App called "Calm" to help me disconnect and meditate for at least 10 minutes daily. Don't forget to write down your observations.

2. Journal one positive experience that happened to you out of trusting your intuition and another negative one that resulted out of ignoring your intuition. Reflect on both scenarios and write the lesson learned for your future.

3. Complete the Gallup Clifton Strengths Finder Assessment by visiting https://www.gallupstrengthscenter.com/home/en-us/strengthsfinder and identify your top 5 dominant themes or strengths. Display those top strengths in a visible area in your office. This will help you become aware of your preferences and make better decisions at work and life to succeed.

Suggested reading for this chapter:

Your chance to excel in what you do increases when you focus on your strengths and work to turn them into unique talents. If you haven't taken the Clifton Strengths Finder Assessment yet, go ahead and do it now. Once you have done that, familiarize yourself with your top themes by reading "Discover Your Clifton Strengths" book and utilizing the tools available in the website to put your unique strengths into actions and create your success story.

"All I do is follow my instincts, because I'll never please everyone."

~ Emma Watson

3
Design Your Future

"Do not go where the path may lead, go instead where there is no path and leave a trail."
~ Ralph Waldo Emerson

You get to live only one life on this earth. There is no second chance or retake. Therefore, you must spend your time here only on people and matters that will make your earthly experience progressive, happy, and meaningful. According to me, the one thing you need to be able to live fully is "courage"; courage to choose what suits you and be responsible for your choices, courage to continue pursuing your path regardless of the negative comments around you and courage to be yourself, do what pleases you and stand out in a world where everyone is trying to wear masks, please others and fit in. The choice is yours! This is what's going to happen when you decide to design your future:

1. Create your future and feel in control…

If your life is a vehicle, then it makes perfect sense that

you sit in the driver's seat and take control of the wheel. Once you are in charge, you have the freedom to design your life plan according to what suits you and create your destiny.

Also, being the driver gives you the flexibility to choose your destinations, the routes you are going to take to reach those destinations or change them altogether when you want to, without the need for approvals from others; as Abraham Lincoln said: "The best way to predict your future is to create it."

2. Stop the blame game...

Being the one who assumes responsibility for your choices, means you will take the credit when things work out, but equally so, the accountability if something goes wrong. It's such a relief for mature people to live like this. This saves them a lot of time and effort that otherwise would be wasted blaming others, the circumstances, or luck, etc.

3. No waiting only seeking...

When you realize that everything in your world starts and ends with you, then you will not sit and wait for the right time, circumstances, or people to grant you permission to make your next move, instead, you will design your life plan and get going. Your life will then be eventful and very productive with remarkable achievements. You won't have time to think of excuses, just opportunities to utilize to their fullest.

4. Make your life experience more fun, thrilling, and meaningful...

It cannot get more exciting than that. You keep on investing the time and efforts to work on your life plan and providing value to others, and life responds by blessing you with great opportunities to maximize your contributions, have fun along the way and increase your contentment day by day. Your life will turn into a field of opportunities where you get to choose what works for you, provided you have the right intent and do the necessary work to deserve such entitlements. Especially in the hotel environment, where no two days are the same, you can imagine the unlimited opportunities that you can get and all the difference you can make if you rise to the challenge.

5. Be a trendsetter and introduce new solutions to humanity...

We all work, but what is it that distinguishes the most

effective professionals from the rest? They talk about things that matter to the world. The highly successful people become successful by discussing the most critical issues in their field of expertise and providing solutions that help humanity on a wider scale. They start by being clear on their own life purpose and aligning it with their organizational priorities. This will have a positive impact on their communities and result in them setting trends as well as providing answers to some pressing questions that serve humanity in their area of expertise.

★★★

Bronnie Ware, an Australian nurse has written a best seller titled, "The Top 5 Regrets of the Dying", which lists the most common regrets she heard from her patients on their death beds. Guess what was the # 1 regret? –

HR Team Photo During My First Job in Burj Al Arab Jumeirah

"I wish I'd had the courage to live a life true to myself, not the life others expected of me." This really means you are the only captain of your ship and the driver of your bus. If you give others the access to your driving wheel, you are already off-track and going to places that are not even close to your original roadmap.

When you realize that your life is almost over and look back clearly on it, it is easy to see how many dreams you let go unfulfilled. It's much easier to follow others and let them plan our life details to escape from accepting responsibility, but the long-term effects of this strategy will be very daunting and pathetic. The majority of people in this world, and many around us have not honored even half of their dreams and many had to die knowing that it was due to choices they had made, or not made. How does thinking about this make you feel already?

The nature of work in hotels and all the non-stop happenings there with colleagues and guests, makes it very possible to forget yourself and drift away from your goals and main life purpose. It gets easy with time to be swayed away by other people's concerns in such service-driven environments and disown your life. I'm here to remind you that you must maintain your focus and stop working in all different directions, as I've come across many people during my hospitality career journey who come to work but don't know their main "WHY!" So, how to beat the odds in this particular aspect to become an exceptional hotelier; is to do what the majority are not doing; design your life map based on your "Why" to stay on purpose, regardless of daily distractions.

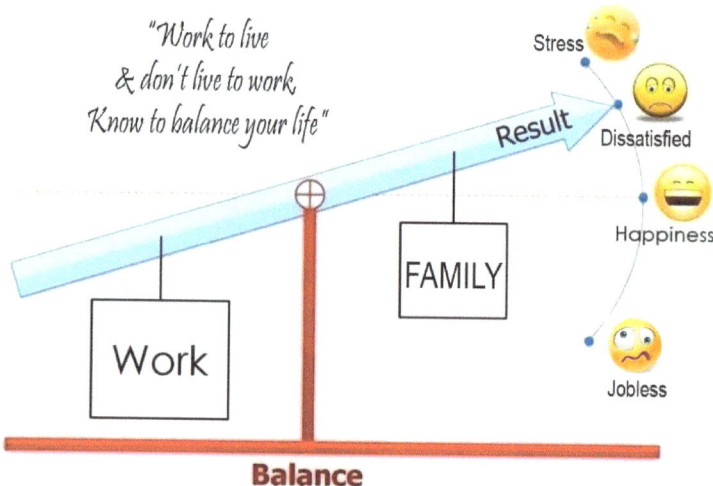

Even though this is the most sensible approach to live your life, why do we see a lot of people around us living in denial and refusing to accept responsibility? The answer is simple! Because this is easier said than done and requires a lot of courage which not everyone has. So here we will examine three concerns people usually raise when thinking about taking responsibility and planning their life:

O1 *What if people around me at home or work don't support my dreams and call me selfish?*

R1 This is one of the most common questions I get from people when they plan to do something new or more aligned with their life purpose. They become fearful about how their family, friends and colleagues will react to such new and sometimes unheard-of plans and ambitions and whether they will still be loved and accepted or not. Honestly, a few years before, I used to have similar concerns too. As social beings, we humans mostly seek approval and acceptance of others and it's an important need that we strive to fulfil especially in the early stages of our careers and life in general (see stages of wisdom in chapter 7). We have such a big need for social acceptance that often we don't mind dedicating or rather wasting our entire life pleasing others and fitting in, even if that doesn't suit us and gives us a lot of pain. With time, as we grow in consciousness and awareness, we slowly understand that pleasing others is not always possible.

During My Participation in LEAD Conference 2017 Dubai

People around us don't understand our dreams and goals, so they may indulge in behaviors that put us down and discourage us. It's very likely that these people are those who one day have decided to scarify their dreams to remain loved by others. One of the common practices they will use is emotional blackmailing. They will threaten you with withdrawing their love and call you selfish and self-centered. That's why, it's very important for you to read chapter 2 and learn the practices that will help you establish stronger a relationship with your inner self and trust your intuition before taking major life decisions. Having a strong focus inward can make you more determined. At that point, you can overlook what others around you think or say and keep pressing forward and focusing on pursuing your real dreams. On the other hand, there will always be people who will get excited for your new plans and dreams; surround yourself with those people and make them your success partners.

After all, if the love of others is conditional then it's not worth wasting your efforts and discarding your own dreams for it. Be in charge of your life, go ahead and do what your heart is craving for and with time, others will also join you to cheer you on.

O2 *My freedom is directly linked to the amount of responsibility and the number of people around me who support my choices. If I decide to beat the odds, I may end up with more responsibilities and less supporters, or I may lose my job altogether…*

R2 If the journey is yours and you must walk through it anyway, you may as well decide to gather enough courage to make it significant and rewarding for you. In fact, what could be more liberating than you having the control buttons over your major life decisions and as a result being the only one to get the credit or the blame? In this case, you can move straight to action once you have identified your goals without the need to seek approval from others.

Of course, I encourage you to consult with your well-wishers and take other opinions but be mindful to do so from subject matter experts who have done similar things and got successful results, not with a relative or co-worker who doesn't know what you are talking about. Unfortunately, many people take advice from the wrong person, then they wonder why it didn't work! Why do you think the majority of people who don't trust their choices, want to have the maximum number of people buying-in or approving their decisions before they move to execution? To give them the credit when things work out? On the contrary, to start the blame game and avoid taking accountability for the consequences. The reason being most of these people come from a very negative mindset and believe that things will mostly go wrong than go right. They neither trust God's plan nor their own capabilities.

So, the bottom line is, the more responsible you are about your life decisions in general, the freer you become. People who refuse to take responsibility are enslaved by other people around them and what others think or feel about something. Studies have shown that most people who suffer from depression are those who abandon their responsibilities, and this is especially true for people who have experienced retirement. Also remember the fewer supporters you have the less interference and approvals you would need to acquire on how to run your life and the sooner you can begin with the necessary actions that will make you do things your way and turn your dreams into reality sooner rather than later!

O3 *What if I really don't have the courage to pursue my dreams because of elements beyond my control like family, culture or simply lack of resources?*

R3 Ask yourself, what could be possible if you do pursue your dreams regardless of the circumstances? Your ambitions and dreams, especially those which you truly long for, are worth taking chances on and serious steps towards to turn them into reality. No matter how strong our circumstances seem to be, or most of the time, we make them appear so, there are always factors that are in your control and you can influence. Think of it this way, unless you take your first step on the staircase, you wouldn't be able to see what lies beyond it. You don't want to start worrying about what will happen in the sixth or the seventh step, while you haven't even made up your mind to take the first step in faith. Life works exactly the same way, focus on your circle of influence and you will, with time, make it bigger than your circle of concern.

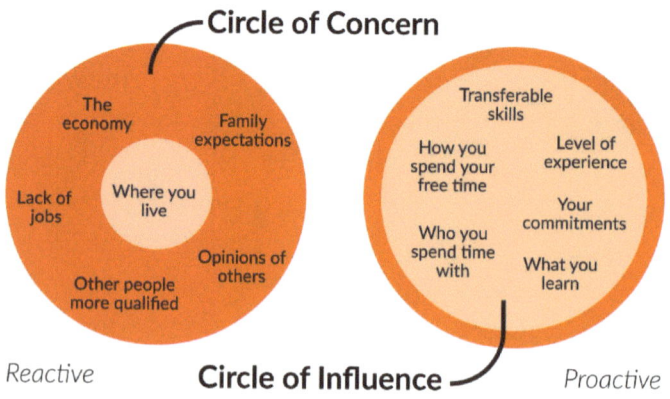

It's easy to make excuses and give ourselves imaginary reasons why something will not work out, but the pain of regretting something we have not done is far greater than the pain of attempting something and failing at it. Now consider the joy and the rewards of pursuing something in spite of the resistance you face and achieving tremendous success at it. Words cannot describe such feelings! I'm here in 2018, rewinding all the challenges that I've faced ever since I decided to take complete responsibility for designing my life and where do I stand today? I'm more confident that my future will be even brighter due to the choices I'm making now. Taking complete responsibility for my life has definitely made me stronger, wiser and more fulfilled. I therefore, invite you too to re-evaluate your current scenario, take some serious and courageous steps towards making your dreams a reality and stop making lame excuses for your current situation. Every day is a new day and you still have a chance as long as you are alive.

Now, after defying some pressing mindset resistance, let me show you three simple steps that will help you get started with identifying your direction and designing your unique life map:

1. Clarify your purpose and stay true and authentic to it.

This is a very serious discussion. If you are a hotelier, then you may be in this industry because you value service, royalty, extravagance, and people. Whatever your values might be, let's agree that most of us chose working in hospitality because it represents something we value.

In our industry, we repeatedly talk about the importance of providing authentic and genuine service to our guests. Most hoteliers even receive a lot of training to equip them with the necessary skills to deliver that excellent service. However, you need to be authentic with yourself first before you talk about extending authentic service to others. Your guests can verify your authenticity through their senses and feelings. Therefore, get the basics right and stop acting.

Furthermore, being on purpose makes your work more exciting as time passes by, because you realize that you are getting closer to your goals day by day. On the other hand, working aimlessly, just because everyone is doing it, becomes very exhausting in the long-term as you feel you are out of alignment with your true being.

It's a unique feeling when you know what you are heading towards in your journey and why. Recall your main motives of choosing the field you are currently working in over thousands of other opportunities available in the market. If recalling your initial motives still fills you with enthusiasm, great! Continue delivering your best work and innovating in your field of expertise. Contrarily, if those reasons don't resonate with you anymore, it means that it's time for you to change and move on to something else that will excite you.

Sometimes such changes are needed, and you will be the only person to know at what point in your life you need to transition from one bus stop to another. There will be many signs along the way that will help you make a right decision.

This is a very natural process of life, we are meant to upgrade our choices as we evolve in our journey and broaden our knowledge base and skill set. We deceive ourselves and play smaller than our capacities when we force ourselves to continue doing the same stuff that we have always done, and this is a big waste of our valuable time on this earth and not fair to others around us.

This may not be anyone's fault, it's just the requirement of your current phase. I recall at one stage in my career, when I was facing non-stop issues in the company I was working at that time, someone told me that sometimes our talents and aspirations become greater than what the current place can contain and thus, the best option in those scenarios is to move on and avoid clinging to one place like it's the end of the world. That sentence was very enlightening because it changed my perspective on how I looked at such situations. After all, if you are really good at what you do, you will shine anywhere you go.

2. Stop acting busy and start being effective!

We've seen most people around us taking pride in being busy as if being busy is a sign of importance and effectiveness! You may know a lot of people in your professional circle who have been busy ever since you've known them, and by now you may have started wondering what exactly keep those people busy or what has been the significant outcomes of them being busy all the time? This may sound very extreme, but were we born to remain busy and then die? What's inspiring about that?

It's very much understandable if someone is busy at the beginning of their professional life, at the start of a new job or during an important project, however, I still don't get the idea of being busy every single day of the year! At some point in my career, I've been equally guilty of this as my other co-workers. But, after long years in this field, I realized that there must be a better way of working as I was getting extremely burned-out from adopting this treadmill approach and working on autopilot.

DID YOU LIVE? DID YOU LOVE? DID YOU MATTER?

Most of our issues start when we attempt to cancel our brains and suppress our emotions. Avoid operating like a machine and pause to reignite your purpose. This will help you remove the insignificant fillers or time killers and redirect your focus to the most important tasks or projects that will contribute towards your growth and effectiveness.

Allow some empty time like two or three 10-minute slots throughout your day to plan better and realign your tasks to serve the bigger picture of your organization as well as your career.

3. Set ADS objectives and break them down into actionable steps.

Once you have sought clarity on your key priorities, it's time to write them down. Writing goals is a daunting exercise for many people, but it has been proven that people who write down their goals regularly, increase the odds of achieving them. What's even more important is to write down those goals in an effective way to help you stay on track and achieve exactly what you want. We have all heard of SMART goals, and that's one common way of writing goals. Another way is to set ADS goals. ADS goals, if done correctly and consistently, will help you drive results, continue learning, and get noticed. You can set ADS goals for any area in your life, not just your career.

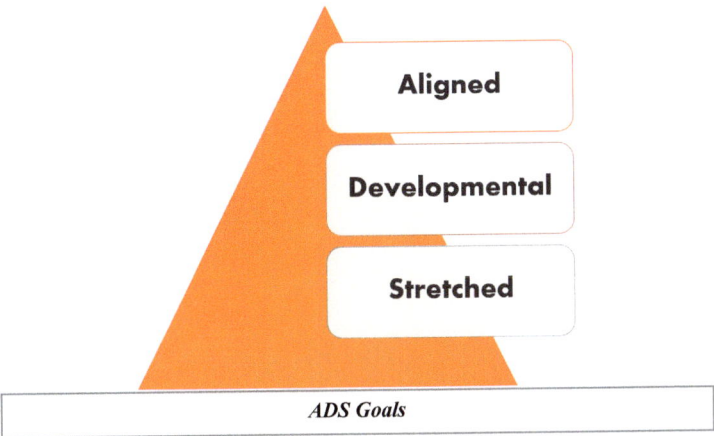

ADS Goals

This exercise is very motivating, and you get thrilled as you tick the boxes of goals achieved! But let me first explain the meaning of ADS:

A: Aligned – Your personal goals must be aligned with your organizational objectives to ensure that you are providing value to your employer and delivering desired results constantly.

D: Developmental – The goals you set for yourself must be developmental and enable you to access new knowledge base and cultivate new skill sets in the process. This will help you to continue learning and build your credibility.

S: Stretched – Your goals must be stretched to ensure that you get out of your comfort zone and navigate in new areas of your field. Expanding your scope and being innovative in what you do will make you noticeable not only for your employer, but also for other best employers if you promote your efforts effectively.

The impact of writing ADS objectives and following through with them can have a profound effect on your career growth and future like the benefits of commercial ADS (advertisements) that promote a product or service, build goodwill, and enhance the brand image in the market to outperform the competition. Keep designing your career plan and highlighting your efforts in this way to increase your professional effectiveness and personal fulfilment.

3 Actions you should take as a result of reading this chapter:

1. Using the Co-Active Coaching's "Wheel of life" shown below, rate your fulfilment in each of the 8 life areas and then connect the dots. See how your personal wheel of life looks like and ask yourself: "If this was the wheel of my life, how bumpy would my ride be?

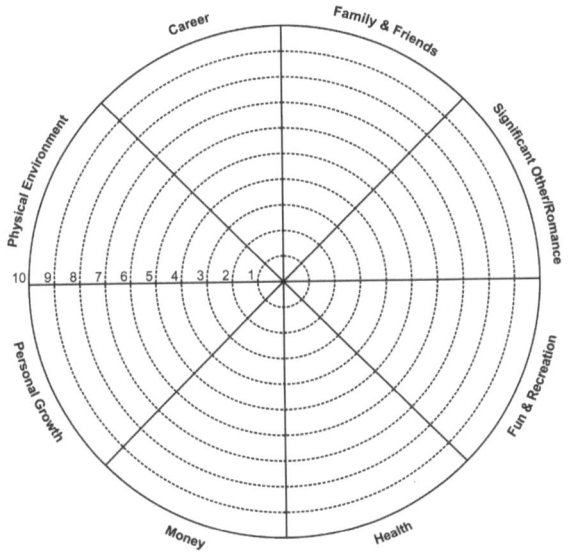

Credits: Co-Active Coaching (3rd ed.) © 2011 by Henry Kimsey-House, Karen Kimsey-House and Phillip Sandahl

2. Now select 3 life aspects shown in the wheel of life that you would like to improve your overall fulfilment with. Decide what score you would like to get to in each area, then set at least 1 ADS goal

for each. E.g. Money: Set aside 10% of my total income to enroll in self-development courses about money management or buy money related books for the next 12 months. (The goal is stretched to save 10% of my income for 12 months, aligned with my value of continuous learning and developmental for me as I will learn new skills).

3. Look at your current job and the role you are performing at your company, and ask yourself: "How is this helping me to get where I'd like to be in 3, 5, 10, 15 years from now?" Write down the answer in a piece of paper and stick it in a visible place next to your workstation. Every time you read this, you will be reminded of why you are doing what you are doing which will strengthen your sense of purpose. People who know they are "on purpose" tend to survive difficult times and thus achieve more than their other counterparts who just do things out of habit.

Suggested reading for this chapter:

Do you know why you get up in the morning? What is it that you have been continuously searching for in this life? Do you know your 'why'? If not, then I suggest you read Simon Sinek's "Start with Why" sooner rather than later. In this book, you will learn that your Why is the purpose, cause or belief that inspires you to do what you do. When you think, act and communicate starting with why, you can inspire others.

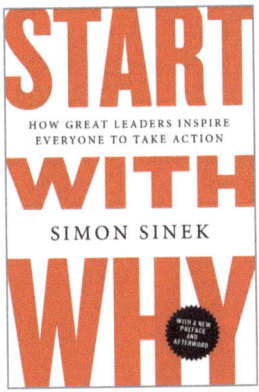

"If you don't design your own life plan, chances are you will fall into someone else's plan. And guess what they have planned for you? Not much!"

~ Jim Rohn

4
Celebrate Your Mistakes

"A person, who never made a mistake, never tried anything new."
~ **Albert Einstein**

We are living in a society which is obsessed by perfectionism and discourages us from making mistakes. Making mistakes is inevitable because we are humans and our mistakes will help us learn and evolve in our lives. Considering that hospitality is a service-oriented industry where you serve people who have different beliefs, tastes and preferences, expecting to get it right every single time is quite impractical. The sooner you start accepting your mistakes as a source of feedback that will move you towards improvement, the happier and more productive you will be in what you are doing. Moreover, making mistakes can help you in a number of ways including:

1. Helps you learn and grow…

Adopting a proactive attitude about mistakes can make a big difference between your success and failure in the long-term. As Stephen Covey says: "*The proactive approach to a mistake is to acknowledge it instantly, correct and learn from it.*" People who become subject matter experts after several years of professional life have all made mistakes along the way and learnt from them. You and I are no different. It's not about being perfect, it's about making progress in the right direction.

2. Teaches you how to forgive...

When you realize that we all make mistakes as humans, this makes you give others the benefit of doubt and avoid dwelling on their mistakes. You will come across as a tolerant person and this will attract your colleagues and manager towards you and encourage them to bypass your mistakes too when they occur. People who know how to let go of hard feelings are happier and more productive in their lives. Be one of them.

3. Helps you discover who you truly are...

The mistakes you make help you identify your strengths, areas of development and what to focus on to bridge your knowledge and skill gaps. You will learn more about your attitude towards failure and whether you are open and flexible to receive feedback following your mistakes, and learn to improve. Your mistakes will also help you discover your passions and how far you are willing to go to master your craft and excel in what you are doing.

4. Encourages you taking risks and pushing boundaries

You will be willing to take more calculated risks and try new things if you are not afraid of failing. Knowing that mistakes are bound to happen at some point will make you less hesitant to experiment in your area of work to improve your results. This will make you deliver your best work day in and day out and achieve more than what you have planned for yourself.

5. Builds your confidence and self-assurance

The more mistakes you make in the early part of your career, the sooner you will have your breakthroughs and learn your stuff. The more effective you become in your field of work, the greater opportunities you will be surrounded by to take you to higher levels of success and increase your confidence in your abilities and potentials. Your self-confidence will lead you to uncharted territories and take you to great places you have never imagined in your life. You will experience this and more if you have the right attitude towards mistakes and trust your capabilities.

★★★

People who don't make mistakes are the ones who are falling behind because they don't take the risk to get ahead. Let's agree that most of our mistakes are not intentional. They just happen due to lack of knowledge or experience in handling people or situations. It's very natural not to get things right at the first shot. You don't need to be guilty about it or let someone around you exaggerate the situation. There is always a first time in doing something. Remember your first job, first interaction with a guest or first report that you prepared for your manager, you may be smiling as you remember those moments because you know they were not as good as they could be, but those were your first steps towards establishing your best work.

If you don't make mistakes, you don't make anything. Your mistakes will push you forward and put you on the right track unlike what many people misguidedly think about mistakes. Imagine spending most your life being very cautious about doing new things, meeting new people, or trying new experiences! Think of all the fun and opportunities you are going to miss with such limited thinking. You will see others around you moving ahead in their lives while you are wasting your precious years clinging to your fears of being wrong or making mistakes. Guess how inspiring it will be to pass on some stories to young professionals later in your career, to tell them that they can certainly succeed if they have a positive attitude towards learning from their mistakes and relate to your early beginnings in the industry. One of the things I always feel proud about when contemplating the latter days of my early professional experience is when I started visiting career fairs, schools and universities to talk to young Emiratis. I tell them about the challenges I went through when I started working in hotels because of my lack of experience, technical skills and knowledge. Despite the mistakes I might have made in my early career, I can pride myself on standing up and acknowledging that those very mistakes are the stepping stones that helped me climb the success ladder and become a well-known expert in my field. No mistakes, no such inspiring stories. The choice is yours!

With Hyatt Team During Participation in Careers UAE 2013

You ought to make frequent mistakes and face difficulties when you opt for new things. There is nothing wrong with that. It's a natural process to prepare you for your best time ahead. After all, this is exactly what's called "experience".

This is very much like what happens to gold. The metal is put through several stages of grinding and excessive heat in order to refine it and turn it into pure gold. Following that strenuous process, this very same metal becomes a precious asset and sold for lofty rates in the marketplace. Likewise, your learnings and experiences will become more valuable in the marketplace after you make a series of mistakes and learn from them during the course of your career.

Mistake increase your experience;
And experience decreases your mistakes.
You learn from mistakes;
While the others learn from your success!

So, how to beat the odds with your attitude towards mistakes? Well, start with accepting the fact that making mistakes is a crucial part of your learning process, then use your judgment to find out the best way to find a solution to the problem created by your mistakes. The more you experiment with different methods and improvise on them, the more success you will achieve in your profession in the long-term.

So, what are the main objections people have about making mistakes? Let's explore a couple of them in this section:

O1 *What If my manager or team members expect perfect work and punish those who make mistakes?*

R1 I'm sure they will understand your reasons as mistakes are inevitable, especially if you are working on something new. You just need to acknowledge your mistake, correct it where applicable and let them know that you will learn from it. After all, they are also humans and make mistakes too. Forgiving and supporting each other will create a workplace that is conducive to learning and providing feedback. Also keep in mind that it will depend on the nature of the mistake. Forgetting to place the amenities in the guest room is a mistake and moving from your place as a lifeguard without a justified excuse is another mistake. It will also depend on the severity of the consequences and will be dealt with according to your company's policies and procedures. In all cases, the learning is what you need to focus on to move forward in your life and not to dwell on your mistakes.

O2 *In my work environment, the more mistakes I make, the less competent I'm perceived as and that limits my chances for growth and promotion. How should I handle that?*

R2 We are talking about making first time mistakes and learning from them, not repeating mistakes; there is a big difference between the two. Besides, what are the chances of you doing something completely new that no one else has done before you at work? I would say, very slim and there is nothing new under the sun anyway. Today, there is a body of knowledge concerning every area of our lives. At work, your manager, senior colleagues, and HR and L&D practitioners will be the best people to ask about how to do something.

Start by looking inside yourself. Maybe you need to enhance your emotional intelligence skills or learn to adapt to constant changes in your work environment. If you are lacking some knowledge or skill set that prevents you from performing your job better, ask for training in those particular areas. Hotels are well known for providing intensive training opportunities for their employees.

Training?

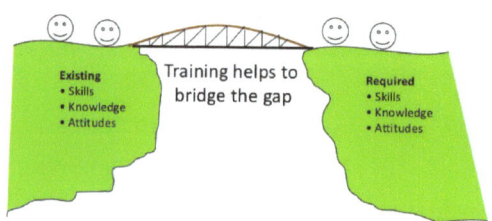

If it's not about training, then you need to question yourself whether you are in the right place. If you are in an environment that discourages people from taking risks and being empowered to experiment and learn, then you are not going to be happy even if you get promoted by any chance. Your actions will be governed by fear and when you operate from fear more mistakes tend to happen. If you are managing people, then they will not be happy either under that management style because they won't be growing.

Q3 *In hotels, we place a big focus on guest satisfaction by attempting to minimize any gaps or errors in the overall guest experience. This means if we make mistakes, the guest will complain, and our guest satisfaction scores will drop accordingly. How to look at mistakes in this context?*

R3 All the big names in service-oriented organizations focus on giving the guest a memorable experience. Having no complaints is not an absolute indication of high service quality. In fact, you need to be worried when you receive no complaints. It could be that your guests are emotionally disengaged, or your employees are actively looking for other jobs in silence. Complaints are a measure that your guests and employees care about your company and would love to see it doing well. Listening to your internal i.e. employees and external customers i.e. guests and suppliers then acting upon their feedback to improve will place your hotel and your own career in a very strong position.

So, it's not about having no complaints; it's "how" you manage those complaints or not when they occur that will ultimately contribute to a positive or negative guest experience.

So, we agree that our perception to making mistakes need to change; now let's examine how to deal with mistakes to make the most out of our experiences in life:

1. Turn your mistakes into opportunities to make a difference.

Start by identifying your childhood conditioning about making mistakes, what your parents, siblings or teachers used to repetitively say or do. Those words or actions contributed to forming certain beliefs or perceptions in your mind about how mistakes directly corelated with safety, punishment, acceptance, and success in life. Being aware of how you were subconsciously programmed, and your inclinations is a big step forward. That's why self-awareness is considered the first step towards being an emotionally intelligent individual, only then can you move on to the next step, which is self-management.

During Participation in Careers UAE 2014 to Boost Emiratization in Hospitality Industry

Don't be reluctant to do new things just to avoid making mistakes or upsetting others. This is your journey and you will know what's most suitable for you. The mindset of being terrified by mistakes will prevent you from living a meaningful life. What you resist persists so don't aim for perfection, rather aim for excellence, and that will only be achieved by continuous learning and improving your results day by day. The sooner you accept your shortcomings as a human being, the better you will feel about yourself and life in general. Moreover, feeling good will enable you to deliver your best work, day in and day out. It's important for you to realize this to avoid being harsh on yourself and move on to the next exciting project instead of dwelling on past mistakes.

2. Use your drawbacks to help others regain confidence in their own capabilities.

Your choices in the early stages of your life will greatly determine your future outcomes and quality of life. When I recall my early career drawbacks and mistakes, and fast forward to 13 years of professional experience, I consider them the greatest blessings that made me what I'm today. Young people and other professionals approach me at this point to learn from my experience and I'm privileged to be able to use my knowledge and skills to coach young talent. I feel honored to transfer my valuable learnings to help them recognize their strengths and apply them in a way that will bring them fulfilment in whatever they do.

Big Sister Talk for the Students of HCT Dubai Women's College in 2014

I've been involved right from the initial years of my career in hospitality in speaking to students about their career options in various forums during career fairs, college, and university symposiums as well as answer their questions from my own experience. I've also started speaking in various conferences to share my career lessons with other professionals and form collaborations that will provide greater benefits to the wider community.

It's very important to have live examples of people who have used their mistakes as stepping stones to create success stories. This will encourage and inspire the coming generation to keep pressing forward and show them that making mistakes is a sign of progress, which is way better than stagnation.

The more we help others gain confidence in their capabilities and potentials, the more successful and credible we become in our life.

3. It's not the mistake, it's what you do about the mistake that really matters.

Receiving Recognition from Dubai Tourism for Supporting Emiratization in Hospitality Industry

People who are hesitant don't go very far in life. Don't be one of them. You are a Hotelier, you are here to challenge your boundaries and create unforgettable experiences for other people. The most impactful experiences for hotel guests are the ones that are spontaneous even if they were imperfect. Those imperfections and small mistakes make guest experiences more human and provide you another opportunity to correct them and exceed your guests' expectations. Adopt this new way to look at your role as a hotelier, wow your guests and earn their loyalty. See how your mistakes in this context, allow you to be a better hotel professional, enable you to build deeper relationships with your colleagues and guests and as a result improve your hotel's reputation.

So, it's not really about mistakes, it's all about what you do with those mistakes and how you turn them into vehicles to progress and impress.

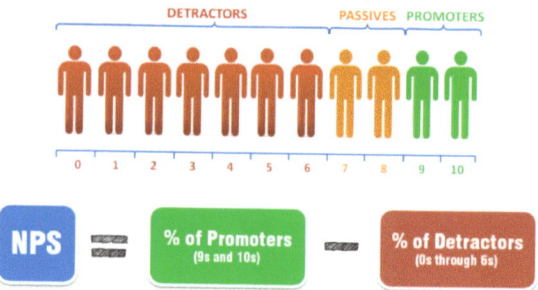

3 Actions you should take as a result of reading this chapter:

1. Make a list of your self-limiting beliefs about making mistakes based on the conditioning you received or your past experiences, in order to be aware of them. Once you have done that, write down the benefits of making mistakes from your point of view and compare both sets of answers.

2. Share with your colleagues (possibly in a team meeting), how one of your mistakes helped you become more confident and less fearful. Explain to them how it helped you to look at things from different perspectives. This will encourage others to share their learnings and create a safe environment for people to admit their mistakes.

3. Identify at least five successful managers and leaders in your organization and request them to talk to you about one of their mistakes, committed in their early career journey, and how they turned it to their advantage to become what they are today.

Suggested reading for this chapter:

When we start our professional life after college, we think we have figured out most of the answers we need to achieve our dreams. Once we are out there, we get overwhelmed and make one mistake after another. Making mistakes disheartens most people and they think of quitting. John C. Maxwell explains in his book "Failing Forward" that the major difference between achieving people and average people is their perception of and response to mistakes and failure. I urge you to read this book if you've not already read it.

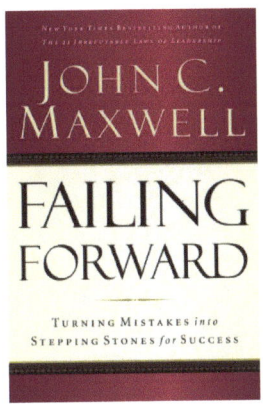

"A life spent making mistakes is not only more honorable but more useful than a life spent doing nothing."
~ George Bernard Shaw

5
Boost Your Credibility

"Education is like a lantern which lights your way in a dark alley."
~ **H.H. Sheikh Zayed bin Sultan Al Nahyan**

The world is changing around us at such a frantic pace that if we do not continue to grow and develop, we will soon be left behind. In the 21st century, we all need to be lifelong learners. We need to continually keep our skills sharp and up to date so that we have an edge in all that we do. Of course, we all have a natural desire to learn, to adapt to change, enrich our lives and fulfil our dreams. Here are five key benefits of learning and constantly upgrading your knowledge and skills:

1. Be more qualified and credible...

Every job has a minimum education or knowledge requirement, for the incumbent to be considered suitable to start working in that job. As time goes by, you need to re-evaluate/update your education, upgrade your knowledge, and continue learning to help yourself advance in your career and qualify for promotions. Further, your commitment to ongoing learning and pursuing further education will show your employer and colleagues that you don't have all the answers, but, you are willing to do the necessary work to learn, which will boost your professional credibility.

2. Help you gain a competitive edge...

Look at the overall workforce in the hospitality industry. How many hoteliers around you, do you think, will be highly educated and really qualified in their fields? From what I've seen so far, not many; only a few. Think of the leverage you would have if you are one of those few; wouldn't it be exciting to be among the very few best ones out there in terms of education and knowledge? This will immediately put you in the forefront and increase your chances of success in your industry and profession.

3. Make more money over a span of your career...

Many studies have shown that highly educated people, and those who are coachable and keen on learning and introducing new ways to improve their work results, build a positive reputation in their profession and increase their chances of being promoted, getting headhunted by the best employers, or receive offers to form joint ventures with top influencers in their industry. This in turn helps them make more money during the tenure of their working life and increase their net worth. In general, the more educated you are, the more valuable your contributions to the table, and that enables you to become richer over time compared to your counterparts.

4. Improve your lifestyle and increase your options...

Being highly educated will fast track your success in life. People generally believe that success breeds money and power. I further add freedom and fulfilment to this list. When you work hard at your education and seeking knowledge, you learn more things. The more you learn the more options you will have in this life to live your purpose and become effective in what you do. You learn that there are many ways to reach the same goal and then you choose the method most aligned to your values and strengths to deliver amazing results and standout from the crowd. People with lack of knowledge look at life from a scarcity point of view, while the learned belief in abundance. Notice how knowledge determines people's general outlook towards life and improves their life quality and options.

5. Become more aware and well informed...

We are living in an age characterized by easy access to information. There has been no better time to acquire knowledge and have readily available information like today, at any time in human history. You have no excuse not to learn and stay current with what's new in your industry and profession. You can get all the information you need at the click of a button. Information is power, knowledge is liberating, and people who know the most are the elite in their fields and in control of their destinies. Be one of them.

★★★

According to a study published by the "The College Payoff 2011", people who pursue continuing education and professional qualifications, on average, have relatively higher lifetime earnings. For instance, a master's degree holder earns more than double the money of a high school graduate. Similarly, someone with a professional degree would earn 60% more than someone with a bachelor's degree alone. In fact, higher education is emerging as a stand-alone industry in many developing countries due to the great focus on and increased global competitiveness

Happy Moments During MBA Graduation Ceremony 2012

for high quality education. Besides, many companies recognize the need for vocational qualifications and make key decisions related to recruitment, promotions and secondment of their employees based on the relevance of their qualifications and knowledge base, to the needs of the market and industry they are operating in. Bottom line, keep learning to stay in the race!

If you can't bear the short-term pain of educating yourself and seeking knowledge, then you've got to bear the long-term pain of being stuck in your job without any evident growth and eventually you may even become redundant because of your outdated information.

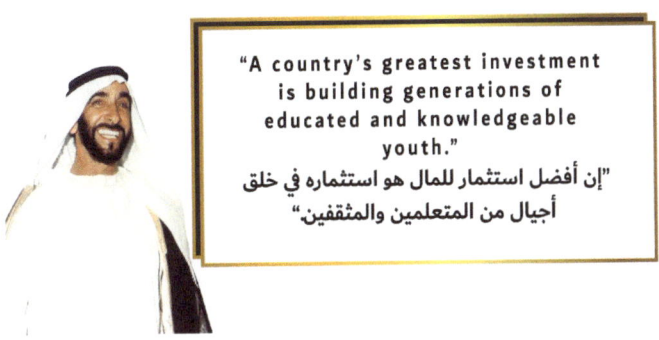

"A country's greatest investment is building generations of educated and knowledgeable youth."

"إن أفضل استثمار للمال هو استثماره في خلق أجيال من المتعلمين والمثقفين."

In other words, you won't be able to stay current with all the new ways and technologies in your industry and profession. Once that happens, you won't be able to excel in your work nor add any value to your employer and you may as well risk losing your job if you are not proactive in learning and improving. Knowledge is power, and the lack of it would most certainly reduce your chances of succeeding and reaching the heights you have always dreamt of in your life.

If you want to last long in your industry and field of specialization and become more credible, then you must continue learning over the span of your life. Whether you choose to acquire an academic degree, earn a professional qualification, or become an active member of a relevant association, the long-term payoff of such decisions will prove beneficial to your career and life in general. As a hotelier, you will beat the odds in this area if you continue acquiring relevant degrees and qualifications related to your industry and profession as opposed to the majority of hoteliers who believe that years of working experience will offset the need for any education. You definitely need the work experience to learn how to apply your skills in practice, but you also need to learn the rules of the game and best practices from the best sources to ensure that you are practicing your craft correctly to become the best!

Internationally Accredited Qualifications That I Have Acquired

And now, let's look at some of the common objections that I've heard when I spoke to professionals around me about focusing on their education and constantly acquiring knowledge:

O1 *What if my employer doesn't support my education and think it will affect my performance?*

R1 Let's first accept that your education will definitely affect your performance but in a positive way. You need to make your manager see the value you will add upon learning and becoming more aware about the best practices in your field, and how this will ultimately contribute to your team's success and make your manager look good. It's really up to you how you sell this to your manager to make him/her see you as a valuable team member and you may as well get more support. However, if your projects lag behind, and your work performance suffers because of your studies, you then need to re-evaluate your priorities and plan how best to go about balancing the two things. On the other hand, if your manager feels threatened from your advancement and further education, then it's your call whether to continue working for such a manager or start looking for other alternatives.

O2 *What if it gets too much for me and I'm unable to cope between work demands, family and study requirements?*

R2 Knowing how demanding it can be to work in hotels with their long working hours, I understand that it may get challenging at times However, I know of many people who work in hotels in operational roles with changing shifts and still managed to further their education. Many of them report that it was not easy but the whole experience was definitely worth it. According to these people, the rewards they have reaped later in terms of personal growth and career success was indisputable. It just proves that where there is a will, there is a way. Once you decide to do it, design a plan on how you will manage yourself and work until you achieve completion. It's always wise to choose to be uncomfortable in the short term, and delay gratification to enjoy the long-term rewards. All successful people have this in common.

O3 *What if I don't have enough funds to pursue a degree or professional qualification in my field?*

R3 Many organizations support and fund the education of their high performing employees. That's why it's important to have a clear goal or career plan to ensure you take advantage of every possible opportunity that is available around you. First, surprise your employer with your hard work and high performance so that they are willing to invest more in you to help you become even better in what you do. I know I did this and it worked for at least two of my certifications. In cases where you have tried and was still not able to secure a sponsorship from your company, your own proper career and financial planning can prove helpful in this matter.

Your other option if you lack sufficient funds for your education is to join relevant professional associations in your field. By paying a nominal annual membership fee, you can have access to unlimited materials, research reports, publications, and get invited to regular paid as well as unpaid workshops, conferences and webinars which will keep you updated about what's happening in your field. You will also get good discounts on the certification programs they offer, so you can pay reduced rates and become certified when the right time comes. In other words, in this age of easy accessibility to information, you shouldn't have any excuse to whine about obstacles to your professional growth. At the end of the day, your career progression is your responsibility, your employer is just a facilitator. Your challenge is to become so good at what you are doing that your contributions cannot be avoided or go unacknowledged.

After we have tackled the objections most professionals have about seeking education and keeping their skills and knowledge current, let's explore how to go about it:

1. Start with the end in mind. How to eat an elephant? One bite at a time.

I don't want to be overconfident and say that I knew exactly what I was doing when I got into the hospitality industry in 2005. It just sounded different and I'm by nature attracted to anything that is unique and non-traditional. So, I started my career with the magnificent Burj Al Arab, where I worked almost 3 years, then what? Then I was fascinated by the idea of being one of the handful Emirati women who had pioneered in the hospitality industry, but how to build that image? I then realized that knowledge is power and remembered a verse from the Holy Quran that says: "God elevates those among you who believe, and those given knowledge, many steps" 58.11. I pondered upon this verse for a while and decided that seeking more education and knowledge is my ladder to advance my professional life and be one of the icons in Hospitality and Human Capital in the region. I weighed my options and decided to step out for a while from my hospitality career to purely focus on my education. I did so because I realized the immense pressure the long working hours in a hotel and the demanding requirements of a dual MBA program with all its group work, assignments and exams would have put on me. However, I did take up a job in a reputed university i.e. Zayed University and worked there while I was completing my MBA and other professional certifications because I had a bigger vision ahead for my career.

A Proud Moment with My Family During My MBA Graduation Ceremony in 2012

Almost four years of education later, being the first one in my family to earn a post graduate degree and achieving the top rank in my graduating batch, I started thinking seriously about going back to the hospitality industry, which I did in the year 2012 when I got an exciting opportunity with

Grand Hyatt Dubai and never looked back. Ever since, I've earned many reputable professional qualifications that have equipped me with the right knowledge and tools to excel in my career and gain credibility. I did all this with an unwavering focus on the bigger picture and taking one step at a time toward success.

2. Know the difference between an academic degree, a certification and a certificate and each ones' value in the job market.

When I started my first job with Burj Al Arab, I attended a lot of great training programs like English classes, train the trainer, group trainer, presentation skills, etc. These courses were very useful for me in my job and helped me improve my performance. However, at that point no one taught me the difference between a degree, a certification, and a certificate. I thought because I had attended all those great training programs in Jumeirah, I'd be naturally recognized in the job market when I listed those courses on my CV! I was quite wrong, as I realized later in my career, there is a big difference between a certificate of attendance, a degree program and a professional certification. This realization was quiet awakening for me and led me to do some research and learn more about the difference between the three. Here is the distinction:

Academic Degrees: This is the most common path that people undertake to achieve a specific educational rank in a certain discipline as per the traditional educational system. This includes the academic Diplomas, Bachelor's, Master's and Doctoral degrees. This requires students to complete a specific number of credit hours and years and understand the theoretical aspects related to the field of study. Students must successfully complete relevant examinations, assignments and group work with the set passing scores to earn the degree.

Certifications: Also called professional or vocational qualification, this is the prevailing trend these days and the most practical from my point of view and experience. The student still needs to attend some classes, submit some assignments, and sit for exams. Once you are certified, you can display a certain letter after your name and that makes you credible in your profession. Professional certifications are practical because you don't have to spend years to obtain them like the academic degrees. Most of them that I know can be completed within 3 to 18 months at the most. They are also pragmatic because you get to know the best practices in the field of your specialization and asked to work on live scenarios or solve real-time issues in your workplace by providing recommendations. In my view, certifications are win-win for the individual and organization as everyone gets something out of it. You need to be aware of the most reputable professional qualifications in your field and get certified. A few examples are CIPD or SHRM for HR professionals, CPA and CFA for Finance professionals, CEC and CMC for culinary, etc. Moreover, if you are looking for generic hospitality certification then it's worth to have a look at The Emirates Academy of Hospitality Management website as they provide some great certification programs accredited by the American Hotel & Lodging Educational Institute (AH&LEI) in addition to their academic degrees.

Certificates: This is everything else that does not come under the categories of academic degrees or professional certifications. It's just a piece of paper that confirms that the person has attended a certain knowledge or skill training session and may be valid only with a certain employer and for a specific period. In my early years as an employee, I was quite proud of having a lot many certificates, but I was quite shocked when I learnt the difference between certificate and certification! For instance, when I attended a "Train the Trainer" session in 2006 and received a certificate of attendance at that point, that certificate was good at that time, but would be of no value now in 2018. This is because the tools, techniques and even some adult learning theories that I'd learned were the best practice then but became outdated with the new theories and tools that have been discovered in the past 12 years. This means, if I'm a trainer and need to stay current in my field, I need to continue acquiring new certifications, attend ATD

Academic Degree VS Certification VS Certificate

conferences and become a member in an internationally recognized body for Learning and Development to learn about the latest developments in my field. This is just one example, and you can apply the same principle in your respective profession whether it's culinary, housekeeping engineering or HR. It's worth mentioning that eCornell is one of the best online certificate programs for hospitality professionals.

So, which route should you take? It depends. My suggestion to you is to first identify what you are trying to achieve; is it merely learning a specific information or skill to immediately apply it at work and improve your outcomes? Or are you aiming to obtain an international accreditation that will give you credibility in your field and set you apart from the competition? Once you have identified your "Why", you will be able to make a better decision about the best route to achieve it.

3. Be ahead of the game by constantly reading and anticipating the trends in your field of work, then get certified in an area that you foresee the most opportunities in.

This is my favorite game; to always come up with something new and stay competitive in my field. A few years ago, I used to read about coaching and how it's an amazing tool to redirect individuals towards their main purpose and help them be aligned and more effective in their organizations. As a HR practitioner, this always seemed the right way to motivate the talented people around me and thus contribute to organizational success.

I decided to become a certified coach. For me, the program along with the certification track was quite intense (mentally and financially) with all the weekly pod calls, individual coaching sessions, and studying for exams while simultaneously working at my busy full-time job. This took me one year of commitment to complete the certification requirements and I still remember those days when I used to be on pod calls while breaking my fast in Ramadan. I knew it was quite crazy, but it was worth it, with all the knowledge and skills that I have acquired which helped me eventually become one of the very few certified coaches in my industry.

If you read any HR trends reports, you will see coaching is an emerging trend that is expected to redefine the terms of performance management. Effective managers will be those who provide real time feedback and coaching to their employees to boost their performance. Similarly, HR practitioners are playing key roles as business partners to coach business leaders and line managers on how to manage their employees. Being a certified coach builds my credibility and expertise in this matter and provides me with more tools to practice my HR role more effectively and benefit my employer.

3 Actions you should take as a result of reading this chapter:

1. Using a paper and pen, make a list of all the degrees and the professional certifications in your industry and area of work. Shortlist the most important ones to you and make a 5 – 10 years plan with timelines of acquiring all those relevant qualifications. Just making the plan on paper will get you excited about your life and get you chasing the first one already. Celebrate your small wins and also when you complete small projects and assignments. Have a big celebration when you achieve the qualification. Reward yourself and do something that will make you happy.

2. Find out what kind of training and educational support your organization provides and what are the pre-requisites to apply for such programs. You may be expected to have a certain length of service or performance level to get in. Your company may also ask you to do a project that benefits the workplace to apply your learning. Start preparing your proposal or business case on why the company should sponsor your education or course and share it with your line manager and the Learning and Development professional in your organization and get their feedback.

3. Anticipate what will be the trends in your industry and field of work 1,3,5,10,15 and 20 years from now by reading the latest industry or professional body's researches and reports. Further, list down the knowledge areas and skills that you need to acquire in order to stay current and remain a competitive and valuable professional when those changes come in your field of expertise and industry.

Suggested reading for this chapter:

Science suggests that the human mind has an almost infinite potential for learning and processing information. In his learning program "Accelerated Learning Techniques", Brian Tracy reveals how you can tap into the power of your mind to learn almost anything you put your mind up to, then employ your learning to increase your career success and prosperity.

"The illiterate of the 21st century will not be those who cannot read and write, but those who cannot learn, unlearn, and relearn."

~ Alvin Toffler

6

Surprise Your Employer

"The real reward for doing your best work is not the money you make, but the leader you become."
~ **Robin Sharma**

In today's fast changing world, it is important that we continue to stay ahead of the curve by thinking out of the box and delivering creative solutions to our employers and tell them through our great work that we are irreplaceable. Companies don't want robots who complete tasks to tick the boxes, they value more those employees who think creatively, help them solve crucial business problems and make them look great in front of their key stakeholders. Your destiny will change when you start looking at your job as your own business and work with your employers as if they were your business partners!

Besides, there are many benefits to showing up at work and delivering your best work consistently such as:

A Proud Moment of Winning The Dubai Quality Appreciation Award for Jumeirah Creekside Hotel Team in 2016

1. Achieve personal fulfilment and satisfaction...

Work is one of the greatest means to achieve personal fulfilment and satisfaction. You feel great when you do your best work because you learn more about your potential and employ your knowledge and talents to serve your colleagues and the company you are working for and help them solve their problems. One of the best feelings is when you go to bed every night and sleep in peace, because you are confident that you have delivered the best work you could that day.

2. Distinguish yourself from the competition...

Give three people the same job and each will carry out that job role quite differently. Your work is your signature, strive to make it a masterpiece. Always think of creative ways to do your job to impress your colleagues and surprise your manager. Do your job so well that people who know you start believing that no one can do that job better than you do. Let your results speak for you and this is the best testimony you can ever get. Work will get tough at times but be persistent and remember that your hard work will never go unnoticed. If it does, then use the techniques mentioned in this book to bring your great work to everyone's attention!

3. Polish your skills and become proficient ...

Malcolm Gladwell talks in his popular book "Outliers" about the 10,000 hours rule, which basically states that you need to practice for 10,000 hours to be proficient in your field. Although this rule has been criticized by many management Gurus, the fact remains that practice makes perfect. You need to stay in your field for a certain number of years to know its ins and outs. You also need to be very mindful to find the right balance between quality and quantity. In other words, where you may need to practice for a certain number of years to get the necessary experience in your profession, you also need to make sure that you are refining your skills, upgrading your knowledge, and acquiring the necessary training along the way to remain at the top of your field.

In other words, ask yourself: "Do I have 10 years of experience or 1 year repeated 10 times?" Be careful of falling into this trap like many other people and thinking that you are a Pro!

4. Impress your employer and be the go-to person...

I say this from personal experience. People who have worked directly with me and experienced the quality of my output can't help but relate to my work. Be so good in what you do that you cannot be ignored. On the contrary, become the first person to come to people's minds when they discuss anything to do with your industry, profession or look for subject matter expertise. I don't necessarily know the answers to all the questions in my field, but unlike many, I do have a strong drive to continuously learn, work hard, and become the best I can be day by day. No matter how hard it may be, I always complete what I start and do that in the best way I can. It fascinates me to touch people's hearts by doing what I do extremely well.

5. Get closer to your next promotion...

A lot of employees shy away from doing anything outside their job description and still expect to be promoted or receive pay raises, purely on the number of years they have been with the company. Sorry to burst your bubble, but it doesn't work this way. When promotional opportunities arise, employers don't necessarily offer them to those who have been around longer with the company or those who are doing barely enough not to be fired! People who stand out in their work, take risks, offer solutions, and exercise leadership will be the ones who progress faster in their careers and get promoted quite often. If you are known in your organization and industry as someone who constantly turns things around and delivers amazing results, then congratulations! Your next exciting project, recognition or promotion may not be far away.

★★★

After more than 13 years of professional experience, I have observed that most people have a very monotonous attitude towards their work. I see most people repetitively doing the same thing over and over just because "it has always been done this way" and resisting to consider new approaches or changes. These are the same people who wonder why they are not being considered for the next promotion!

The hospitality industry in the UAE is known to be very vibrant and volatile. The bright hoteliers recognize this fact and will constantly strive to upgrade their skills and knowledge to be able to meet, or rather, exceed the changing demands of their profession and stay current.

The only constant in life is change. If you don't make efforts to develop and grow you will indeed go backwards. You may be unintentionally damaging your career progression if you are refusing to look at things from newer perspectives and are unwilling to experiment with more effective methods to complete the same old tasks.

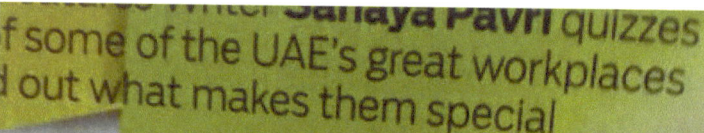

...writer Sanaya Pavri quizzes some of the UAE's great workplaces [to find] out what makes them special

Pictures: Supplied

[B]rian D'Souza
[C]hief Concierge,
[M]arriott Hotel
[Al] Jaddaf, Dubai

[W]ith the company [fo]r 18 years

At the Marriott, the comfort of our guest is the top most priority. It is this inherent sense of hospitality that is ingrained in the company, which makes it a great place to be a hotel chief concierge. The pace is gruelling and hectic and that is what I like the most about my profile. The fact that there is no set routine is what makes it so challenging. The group's new and trendy approach as a brand seamlessly blends work and play in a mobile and global world. And really what makes this a great place are the people I work with who inspire, motivate and support me.

Mona Al Hebsi
Human Resources
Manager, Hyatt

With the company for two years

Hyatt never makes me feel like I am working as every single day presents a new and diverse experience where I can learn, grow and mature. The best thing is that all my colleagues live and breathe this culture daily. We assist one another in achieving our goals.

Each person I interact with, be it a colleague, guest or supplier inspires me with the passion of service I have developed with Hyatt. The organisation offers the perfect combination between work and fun. Employees enjoy being at work because of the full spectrum of social, community and sports events organised for all associates.

Sangya Gurung
Senior Sales
Consultant, THE One
Fusion, Dubai

With the company for six years

The fact that THE One's core purpose is to change the world through ethical sourcing, challenged employees and local volunteering gives me the opportunity to make a difference every day. I am lucky to be a part of it. THE One has empowered me and I have benefited from the training sessions that have boosted my confidence to move up within the company. I have been provided with support and can say that THE One has guided me on a successful career path. Benefits such as medical insurance being extended to our family is incredible. We get 40 per cent staff discount — that's exceptional.

Featured in Gulf News After Hyatt Hotels Dubai Won Great Place To Work In The UAE 2013

You will be hindering your company's success and team members' development if you are set in your old ways. With time, your knowledge will become obsolete, your career growth will stagnate, and your contributions to team success will deteriorate. Once your performance level drops, it clearly shows that you are disengaged at work and you may as well be made redundant. This is certainly not what you'd want for your hospitality career and that's exactly why you need to be dynamic and remain competitive throughout your professional life cycle. Just remember, you are either green and growing or ripe and rotting, choose which one you want to be.

Doing things differently in the hotel industry means observing and noticing the arising needs of key stakeholders and taking innovative steps to fill those needs. It's not about following everyone else, it's about thinking outside the box and being open to exploring new ways of fulfilling your tasks and solving the prevailing issues in your workplace. The more unique the solutions you propose the greater value you will add to your organization. Aim to constantly surprise your manager and colleagues with your unique ways of carrying out your work and stay away from doing things just for the sake of doing them. Do what the majority fail to do; and you will beat the odds in this particular aspect of your career.

Featured When Jumeirah Group Has Won the Dubai Human Development Award 2006 for Emiratization

If the outcomes are so rewarding, why are a lot of employees doing just average work in their jobs? Let's explore some of the concerns that employees might have regarding this aspect:

Q1 *What if my employer rejects all my ideas and says no to everything?*

R1 Notice your own thoughts; it is your own fears that are coming up and keeping you from delivering your best work. I'm pretty sure that there is always something you can change to the better in your workplace, no matter how small that might be. No one is asking you to drive big changes if those are not part of your main job duties, however, you can always discuss with your manager your proposals and understand his/her reservations. Having that conversation will provide the opportunity for both of you to clarify and ask questions.

My Happy HR Team in Jumeirah Zabeel Saray
After Running A Successful Employee Event 2018

There is no reason why your manager will refuse new ideas that can contribute towards improving the quality of work produced in your department and make him look good in front of his manager. Just ensure to highlight in your discussion "what is in it for him/her?"

O2 *I work in an entry level job within the hotel and I believe that creating impact is the role of the senior employees not mine.*

R2 Every role exists in the company to create an impact. Think of the entry level roles in any hotel; Room Attendants, Stewards, or Receptionists; what happens if you take these roles out of the organizational structure? Do you think any hotel can run with unclean rooms, dirty dishes, or unattended guests? You are creating an impact whether you decide to do your job extremely well or not. The only difference is that you create a positive impact when you decide to deliver your best work.

In reverse, you are creating a negative impact and image about your company and yourself when you decide to offer mediocre work. You surely don't want to be the weakest link in such a competitive industry, then complain that you are stagnant in your career or you don't get opportunities for growth and promotion. After all, if you are planning to move up the ranks to more senior roles in the future, you need to start behaving in that way from now!

O3 *The best companies have huge budgets that enable their people to do more.*

R3 This is a misconception. When someone doesn't want to do something, such excuses start surfacing. Let

Winning GCC Best Employer Brand Awards 2016 for Successful HR Interventions Ran in Jumeirah Creekside Hotel

me tell you that in most companies' budgets are just formalities; purely numbers on papers that may not even materialize as stated. The sooner you accept this reality, the better for your peace of mind and career progression. I once worked for a hotel where we were not supposed to spend money on almost anything you can think of. Life didn't stop there, and we were still accountable for the end results and tasked to run top notch employee engagement initiatives to increase our engagement scores, reduce our turnover and show continuous improvements.

Successful 45th UAE National Day Celebration for Jumeirah Creekside Hotel Colleagues

Sure, having money could have helped in big ways, but you will see most hotels aiming to operate on a skeleton budget and promoting cost containment. Not to say that this is the best way to operate a business, but it is the reality. Back to my story, throughout my professional journey, I've worked with several teams who have come up with amazing yet cost efficient initiatives for the business. Hotels in general have very limited budgets and for that very reason, we had to think of creative ways and count on the resourcefulness of our colleagues and our professional network to run effective HR interventions. On occasions of budget cuts, our employees had to be the photographers, DJs, interior designers and magicians! The process of bringing all these talents together was tough but the rewards were definitely worth it. As a result of such collaborative efforts, we managed to show a year on year increase in our employee engagement scores and reduction in employee turnover. When there is a will there is a way. Bring out your creativity and resourcefulness in such challenging times and create miracles!

So, you will say, now that I am convinced about the importance of surprising my employer with my extraordinary work, how exactly do I do that? And I'll tell you that you can do that in three important ways:

1. Start with your own department and be kind to your immediate co-workers...

There is a popular proverb that goes "Charity begins at home" which means that the person's first responsibility is towards his/her closest circle. If you are a working professional in hospitality, then you are likely to spend more time with your team members than your own family. This makes it crucial to exert efforts to create a happy and engaged workplace and bond well with your colleagues. Fortune has published an article that reveals that happy employees are 20% more productive than their counterparts. Don't wait for your co-workers to change; be proactive and take the initiative to improve your work environment for everyone's benefit. Notice the energy of the place and the most common complaints, then take necessary steps to bring people together and help them connect and resolve those issues.

With Jumeirah HR Colleagues During The Global HR Retreat 2016

In the first few years of my career, I worked in an environment that I considered very static. In other words, people there used to be quite serious, merely coming to office to complete their tasks with minimal interactions with each other. As I was in an entry level position at that time, I observed the scenario for quite some time without doing anything about it. Day after day, month after month nothing really changed. After waiting for a long time, I decided to do something about it. I spoke to my manager at that time and proposed to do monthly gatherings for team members to celebrate any birthdays, special occasions or give recognition to any accomplishment achieved during that month. She was a bit hesitant but said let's try it and see how it goes. The first month we did it, everyone came to the room where I'd organized some snacks and beverages and I explained the objectives of these gatherings. It sounded like a good idea, but the first meeting was a bit awkward as people were not used to it. The next month it went much better and we celebrated some achievements and birthdays and gave people gifts. As time went on, people started looking forward to this monthly gathering as it brought us together and made us talk. Eventually to make it more engaging we brought food from home and it was a great idea as food is always known to bring people together. The bottom line here, whatever your position is, you can take the first step and make a difference; where there is a will there is a way.

2. Align yourself with your business priorities and stay focused...

One of the most motivating factors at work for most individuals is combining their efforts with others in the right direction to eventually achieve desired organizational goals. You need to be very clear about how your day to day work contributes to the bigger picture of your company. Ask yourself: what are my hotel's key priorities and business targets? What are the things within my responsibilities that if done well, will help my hotel achieve those targets? We see people around us, busy and running around all day, but there is a big difference between "being busy" and "being productive."

Jumeirah Zabeel Saray HR Team Making Colleagues Happy During the International Happiness Day 2018

I always tell my team members that the criteria for me to assess their effectiveness is to see them putting efforts in the right direction and progressing closer towards the target day by day. I'd rather have them doing fewer things but doing them really well. For example, within my capacity as Director of HR in my hotel, I'm in charge of conceptualizing, designing and driving effective people interventions with my HR team and senior executives in the business. This is important to create a happy place to work for my employees and ultimately increase the overall engagement scores in the annual survey. Therefore, I keep my HR team members focused on driving meaningful internal programs that will help us move the needle on key engagement drivers like recognition, management development, learning and development, etc.

3. Understand your job role and make the most out of it.

In any organization, there are several job roles based on the need of the business. Especially if you have been working for a specific company for quite a while, you will have a good idea about the organizational structure and job roles there. Every job role is made of two key aspects, Job Duties and Job Authorities.

Job Duties are the tasks and responsibilities that you will find within your job description. You must read your job description and fulfil the responsibilities mentioned in it well, to be successful in your job assignment.

Job Authorities are the inherent or delegated power of a particular job role. This power enables the job incumbent to command a situation and utilize resources in a way that is deemed beneficial for the business. Not to forget, such authority is always accompanied with equal responsibility for the outcomes as well as failure to take the right action in a given situation. Of course, the job authorities get higher as you climb the ranks. You will get a better idea about the authorities you have within your role from your job description or line manager.

As a working professional, it's important for you to understand these concepts to work more effectively. Throughout the years of my professional experience, I've noticed a trend which has made me curious. I see the majority of people in my industry working very hard and delivering amazing work, but even after many years, they seem unable to go any further in their careers. What's the issue here?

In my opinion, it's maintaining the balance between Job Duties and Job Authorities. Carrying your duties well will get you only halfway, the other half will happen when you learn to exercise your job authorities where needed. Many people, either because of their lack of understanding of this formula or lack of confidence miss this point and get stuck in their careers. Of course, being someone who only tries to exercise authority on others, without

Running Various Engagement and Developmental Activities for Emirati Colleagues in the Hotel

showing any results, is also a failed approach. That's why I always talk about maintaining the balance.

Another thing I'd like to point out here is that you need to keep yourself updated about relevant laws, policies and disciplines that will help you fulfil your job role well. For instance, you don't necessarily have to be working in Human Resources to develop your understanding about local labor laws, company policies, and relevant disciplines like organizational behavior to understand work setup in organizations. It's your obligation to learn this if you are serious about your career progression and mainly because a majority of your work as a hotelier involves constant interaction with people, especially as you grow in your career and hold managerial ranks. Your employer will value you more if you know more and you will become irreplaceable. Even if you leave the place or industry at some point, the amazing work that you have delivered over the years, will make sure you are remembered long after.

3 Actions you should take as a result of reading this chapter:

1. Next time you walk into your workplace, observe the work environment, and talk to several colleagues to understand what's going on. Further, identify your department's biggest issues and figure out how you can help solve them through your daily work. Create a plan, timeline it and discuss it with your manager. You have no idea how pleased your manager will be to see you bringing solutions to

help him/her solve the existing problems. Once that is done, simply execute your plan and constantly measure its impact.

2. Brainstorm ten different ways of how you can create a notable impact in at least one of your company's key priorities in the Balanced Scorecard. Start implementing at least one new idea per quarter with the help of your team members. Alternately, you can involve the business excellence specialist in your hotel, as well as members from other departments if you require functional expertise.

3. Read your job description carefully to understand your job duties and your job authorities within your current role. Think of ways to deliver your job duties in a WOW manner, instead of just ticking the box. Exercise your job authorities to bring positive improvements to your workplace that will make your colleagues and manager happy and help you demonstrate your leadership skills.

Suggested reading for this chapter:

Break free from your confusion and be more aligned with your faith, values, and principles, whether you are at work or outside it. Larry Julian reveals in his book "God is My CEO" that the most effective and value adding leaders in any organization are the ones who do their work following God's principles and this approach makes them very successful and more likely to achieve the company's financial results.

"Every job is a self-portrait of the person who does it. Autograph your work with excellence."

~ Anonymous

# 7
Shout Your Success

"It's a lonely place to be when you are building your ship. But when you do it, and you set sail, people will see how beautiful and majestic it is."
~ Rebecca Rebouche

What distinguishes successful people from the unsuccessful ones is that they are more comfortable highlighting and talking about their success stories than the rest of the population. Of course, these success stories will include a trail of mistakes and setbacks before it eventually becomes what it is. What's even better is that they know exactly how to share their stories in a way that will earn them credibility and compel their audience to seriously contemplate over what they have just said, done, or written.

Sharing your journey, drawbacks and accomplishments can help you on many fronts such as:

1. Offer opportunities for others to help you...

Talking enthusiastically about your story, previous

hurdles, and future aspirations helps people connect with you emotionally, and they will be eager to support you wherever possible throughout your journey to help you reach your destination. Of course, there will be others who won't be as glad of your success, and that's a normal aspect of life; learn to ignore this category. The good people though, will advocate for you in their networks and promote you however they can. Here, I deeply express my gratitude to every person who has shown camaraderie to push me to be what I'm today, even for their smallest acts of kindness or sometimes otherwise, for my benefit. I remember some people being very joyful when I announced my new book for instance and sending me congratulatory notes to motivate me. I specifically admire those people who were very happy to endorse me and my work in this book, they really have hearts of gold. The bottom line is, I wouldn't have got all this support if I myself didn't take the first step towards it and on occasion asked others to help.

2. Appreciate your tough life experiences and share lessons learned...

When you start telling the world your story, you learn a lot about yourself during this process. You understand your passions, fears, and strengths. With time, you will become better at telling your story, adjust your style and create your own voice accordingly. For example, when I started opening up to people about my past experiences, I noticed that there were elements in my story that I was not comfortable sharing because it caused me pain and as a result, made me emotional. Looking at these experiences objectively, showed me that they carry the most weight in my story and also that other people would hugely benefit from hearing these experiences. So, it was not a good idea to be discreet about those facts and keep them to myself. As time passed by, I learnt how to disconnect emotionally from those events. I still appreciate their occurrence in my life and they constitute an integral part of who I'm today, however, I don't have to keep going in the past and living those moments again with all the painful emotions. I just focus on the lessons learned and that's what you also need to do to move ahead in life.

3. Inspire others and open them up to share their stories too...

As mentioned earlier, stories are very powerful and inspiring. All our lives are a series of stories and people love listening to them, so you just learn how to tell your stories to others to share benefits and evoke transformation. Like many other facts in life we know but don't necessarily apply, sharing our own story is no different. What prevents people from sharing such personal details with others is their fear that they will be judged for their mistakes and be vulnerable. Well, let me tell you, the good news is we all have such moments in our lives and no one is perfect. I've put the chapters in a certain order in this book for a reason. If you trust your intuition (chapter 2), have a life plan (chapter 3), then learn it's ok to make mistakes (chapter 4), acquire knowledge to know the best practices in your field (chapter 5) then go and apply your learnings to impress your employer and achieve great things (chapter 6), you definitely have a story worth telling others (chapter 7). The following chapters teach you how to use your story to build your personal and professional brand and how to combine all these elements together to live a fulfilled life.

Receiving Recognition for Exceptional Performance from Dr. Suliamn Al Jassim, Former VP, Zayed University in 2011

Telling your story will encourage others to step forward and share their stories too. We all have stories to share, it's just that some are willing to go out of their comfort zone and spread the learnings so that people can benefit from them, and others prefer to be comfortable, keep things to themselves, then wonder, why am I not getting much from life? Once people become willing to share their stories, we will have a society whose individuals are comfortable in their skin, accept their limitations, realize that life is a process of continuous learning, and understand that sharing stories with others is the most effective way of learning.

4. Earn credibility in your field and area of work...

Look at all the great leaders and gurus in history, what is the one thing they all did to earn credibility? Right, they shared their stories with the world. You don't actually need to get your biography written if you are not ready for it now, however, you can always write articles, and blogs or talk to your audience about how you solved a particular problem. You can bring new perspectives on topics related to your industry and profession to help others see one situation from different dimensions and hence give them many more options to approach a particular problem. If you seek to make other people's lives easier as a result of your contributions, God's fairness entails that your life will become easier. You will earn credibility and have tremendous success in your area of specialization and your life in general because of your wholeheartedness.

5. Help you for your next promotion or new job...

Having the courage to share your story will contribute towards building your personality and extending your influence. It will establish your credibility and showcase you as a subject matter expert in your field of work. Ask yourself: "what could be possible if other people like clients and potential employers believe that I have the solutions to their problems?" You may be well on the way towards your next promotion or exciting new job. Congratulations! You were willing to put the courage, time, and efforts to do what around 90% of people on this planet aren't doing i.e. sharing their stories and therefore, you deserve to reap the rewards.

★★★

Studies have revealed that sharing stories that contain one identifiable character or single hero, has more impact on the audience than stories that have several characters or just statistics. Stories that are led by one character proved to instigate desired actions from the audience, question existing practices and therefore, evoke transformation in society.

If you shy away from talking about your successes, you will be missing great opportunities to add value and make an impact. Even if you consider what you have done so far ordinary in your view, the learning that it might provide others taking the same journey could be significant to them to reach their goals. Holding the information to yourself can be quite selfish and meanwhile another determined individual who is more open about sharing his/her life experiences will take the lead and seize all the opportunities that you could have gotten if you were more candid in sharing your stories and learnings with the world.

When you're comfortable with who you are and what you've achieved, you'll feel worthy of your success, and you'll feel less awkward talking about your accomplishments. This is especially true in the hotel industry where you get countless opportunities to share your life experiences and highlight your successes due to the distinctive number and prominent profile of peoples you are interacting with on a daily basis. This is beside the interesting nature of work in hotels where there is so much happening every day and no two days are the same. When you come across a colleague or guest during your workday ask yourself; who else does this person know who is in desperate need to know what I know and as a result, connect me to my next break that will get me closer to my goals?

The main question here is: "What keeps people from sharing their stories?" Let's explore some of the common objectives and responses in this area:

Q1 *What if I have many achievements, but I'm very shy to talk about them in front of other people?*

R1 The best way to start is by writing. Early in my career, I started sharing my experiences and humble achievements with the world by writing about them in different forums. This has set the stage for me and gave me more confidence to share as more people started interacting with me and writing back in response to my articles in professional networks like LinkedIn, for instance. Talk about the facts and showcase the challenges you have faced and the mistakes you have made along the way and how you overcame them and what you learnt from your experience. This makes your story more real and relevant to the people who are in a similar stage in their lives and looking for solutions to their problems.

Featuring My Success Story During the Visions2Reality Conference 2016 in the Opening Video

Refrain from bragging, at the same time, avoid being too modest while talking about your accomplishments or you will just sound inferior. Find the balance in everything you do in life. Another technique is to mention others who have helped you in your journey and appreciate their contributions and roles in your success. If you continue writing consistently and benefiting other people, you have no idea how soon people will start looking at you as a role model and an expert in your field. Sharing is always a form of caring, so keep doing it.

O2 *What if I have many doubts? Anyway, who would be interested in knowing about my struggles, mistakes, or accomplishments?*

R2 Be careful, this is your saboteur. Don't let it discourage you from being your best possible version. You can't be on your way to success until you are comfortable with yourself and are willing to contribute and add value. It's not about you alone, neither it is about others. It's about identifying which 'stage of wisdom' you are in presently and how to make the best out of your current stage. Read this chapter further to learn more about what I mean by "Stage of Wisdom."

You've got to feel that you have a responsibility to keep going and contributing your learnings from the current stage in order to get to the next one. You will be surprised to know how many people on this earth are craving to spend time and money to access the knowledge that you have acquired over the course of your life. This is exactly what authors, speakers and consultants do; they trade their acquired life wisdom, knowledge, and experiences to help other people solve their problems by providing them with the right formula and hence save them a lot of time, money, and unnecessary efforts. You can also do the same if you have the right mindset.

Launching Soul Beats @ UAE, The First Publicly Authored Book Featuring Success Stories of Ordinary People in UAE

Q3 Once I share my story I'll be expected to maintain my track record and continue feeding it with further accomplishments. What if this creates more pressure on me to keep up with other people's expectations?

R3 This is a valid concern that I personally used to worry about a lot. First of all, you are doing this for yourself before others. You cannot do anything for others before you do it for yourself. You can't be independent before having been dependent first, neither be interdependent before setting the stage to be independent. Read further to identify which stage you may currently be in and why it matters to grasp this concept. So, forget about other people's expectations of you, fulfil your own expectations from yourself first.

All Winners During Hotelier Middle East Awards 2015

As for the part about pressure to constantly feed your accomplishments, this is the natural process of learning and growing in life. First identify your priorities, then go for turning them into realities. You must strive outside your comfort zone and be willing to take calculated risks to achieve great things in life. The pressure accompanying this is a key success ingredient that will eventually turn into a source of joy to make you proud of telling your story to inspire others.

Let's talk now about how to go about shouting your success and spreading your story:

1. Highlight your challenges and how you turned them into accomplishments.

Start by writing about your obstacles, mistakes, and disappointments and how you have transformed them into vehicles to create your success story. That's how most interesting and inspiring stories go about. Don't shy away from showing your vulnerability. It makes you more human and allows other people to easily connect with you and relate to your experience.

I wonder how most people got things so contrary in their minds, or perhaps this was the way they were programmed since their early childhood. Being open about your vulnerability is what will show others your strengths and inspire them, wearing masks will not. If you try to give everyone around you the image that things are always perfect in your life and you know everything then you are painting an unrealistic picture and creating an instant disconnect with people. On the contrary, when you tell them about your humble beginnings, your struggles, and the mistakes, then this will make your story more interesting, establish connections with those listening to your story and then get them more excited to know how things turned around for you and what helped you achieve success. It's just human psychology and the fact that we all crave for happy endings, exactly like in the movies. Movies present a series of events and difficult scenarios that the hero/heroine or protagonist has overcome and ultimately achieves tremendous success and a happy ever after ending. It's totally up to us to create happy endings in different stages and aspects of our lives by learning the right methods.

In 2015, I gathered courage and published excerpts of my life on LinkedIn. I was quite terrified about it and didn't know how the response would be or even whether it was right to put such personal things out there for everyone to read. As I started writing my first article I was very particular about what to write and how to write it and I was making it difficult for myself. After a few hours of battle between my heart and my brain, I decided to open my heart and put it out there. The moment I decided I don't care, it made all the difference.

When I pressed the publish button on LinkedIn, my heart started beating extremely fast. I was waiting to see people's responses. In a very short time I started receiving likes and encouraging comments from people in my LinkedIn network and others and this is my most viewed article in LinkedIn titled "Empower Yourself Through

Education and Self-Belief". I was very humbled to see people's responses and great cheering towards my first story published in public and this has inspired me to continue writing and urge everyone I know to share their own stories and be proud of them.

2. Understand your current stage of wisdom and how to employ it to make a positive impact.

Real success isn't just about what you accomplish in your life; it's about what you inspire others to do as a result of your accomplishments. If you have read Stephen R. Covey's all time classic "The 7 Habits of Highly Effective People", you'd have learnt about the concept of dependent, independent and interdependent. This is what I refer to as "stages of wisdom" in this book and it's very important to review these three stages here to help you better understand how identifying your current stage of wisdom will enable you to build your success story by inspiring others through your actions. You can apply these stages to assess various aspects of your life, however, we will concentrate here on how you can utilize these to drive your career success. It depends on you and the efforts you are willing to expend to determine how long you stay in each stage of your career.

Let's start with **"Dependence"**, being the first logical stage. In general, the first 3-5 years in your career is your foundation years, when you are mostly dependent on your manager and co-workers to train you on the necessary knowledge and skills, and help you obtain experience to establish your professional life. You are also dependent on your salary to buy key necessities but do re-invest the remainder on your personal development. It's a good idea to be patient and show conformance during the dependence stage because your focus is to polish your skills, gain experience and fund your developmental activities. In this stage, you are giving others the opportunity to coach and mentor you as well as giving them an example of a passionate hotelier under progress.

Then you move to **"Independence"**, which is your next career wisdom stage. You should ideally get into this stage by your 6th year of professional experience and allow yourself several years after that to show consistent performance and earn professional credibility. By this time, you would typically be promoted to a supervisory or managerial role based on your great track record, knowledge and skill set and ability to work independently, as well as manage individuals in your team to perform and deliver results. This will be the stage where you can capitalize on the power of teamwork to deliver outstanding results and achievements and become an icon in your profession and industry. You would need to focus a lot on this stage to develop young talent working in your team and concurrently promote your achievements. The following chapters will give you some guidance on how to do that.

So, once you have positioned yourself as a subject matter expert and established trust with people on the value you can add in your field, then the very logical next thing to happen is that you are going to receive a lot of queries, requests for providing advice, guidance or sharing knowledge so that others can benefit from

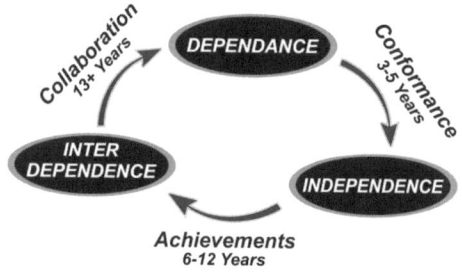

Stages of Wisdom Cycle

your experience. This means now it's your turn to give back, help others and collaborate to create solutions to existing professional or societal problems. We are talking here about the 3rd stage of wisdom; "**Interdependence**." I mapped this cycle on my own professional life and determined the approximate time one should spend in each stage. Of course, at the end of the day this will vary from one individual to another according to their efforts and results, but I believe that you should start giving back and adding value to your profession and society once you've completed 10 years in your career.

3. Show up and turn the impossible to possible.

Getting there is not at all easy. But at the same time, it's not impossible either. Even the word "Impossible" is there to tell you "I'm Possible" if you choose to look at it differently! 80% of success comes from "showing up and making your voice, your voice." It's your continuous hard work and the timely tackling of the un-sexy stuff in your life, that will contribute to creating the sought-after story that you will be proud of telling others. After all, the people who work hard get found.

Delivering Inspire Trust Session to Managers in the Hotel

Creating my place and proving my capability in an industry like hospitality was not so easy. I made sure to show up, deliver my best work and face the scenarios that needed resolutions in different phases of my career. I don't like sweeping pressing issues under the carpet or pretending that they don't exist, otherwise I'd not have been so effective in what I do. I've dealt with different people across all backgrounds and levels, and that made me more experienced and honed my people skills. I've also handled various difficult scenarios at work, but those have revealed my hidden potential and made me even better at sorting out such problems. I've learnt with time that every challenge contains an opportunity and that there are no losses, only gains.

3 Actions you should take as a result of reading this chapter:

1. Make a list of all the things that you have achieved from the time you went to school till date. Write it down even if you feel it's a small thing. Your saboteur may intervene to disturb the process, but don't listen to your negative thoughts. Keep writing to see how much you have already accomplished and be proud of your achievements. Place this list in a visible area i.e. bedside, workstation, or fridge to give you positive vibes and inspire you to achieve more.

2. Think about the mediums through which you plan to share your first success story with the world. Will you start your own blog or use professional network sites like LinkedIn? Write up your first article using the guidelines mentioned in this chapter. It doesn't have to be a long one. The whole purpose of this exercise is to encourage you to share an aspect of your life or work with others to boost your confidence and inspire those who will read your story. Ask a trusted friend or colleague to proofread the article then go ahead and publish it.

3. Identify which stage of the wisdom cycle i.e. dependent, independent or interdependent you are currently in from a career point of view. Write down the reasons why you think so and what gaps

you need to fill to move to the next stage. Draw up an action plan and go for executing it.

Suggested reading for this chapter:

In his book "The Luck Factor", Professor Richard Wiseman identifies the four simple behavioral techniques that have been scientifically proven to help you attract good fortune. He answers some key questions like: Why do some people lead happy, successful lives whilst others face repeated failure and sadness? What enables some people to have successful careers whilst others find themselves trapped in jobs they detest? And can unlucky people do anything to improve their luck—and lives? Reading this book will change the way you define luck.

"One of the greatest experiences in life is achieving personal goals that others said would be 'Impossible to attain'. Be proud of your success and share your story with others."
~ Robert Cheeke

8

Leverage Social Media

"Having a solid, consistent but authentic personal brand online puts you ahead of the competition professionally."
~ Jasmine Kent

What is the first thing you are likely to do when you want to gather information or get to know more about a company, a product or an individual? You will most probably Google them? Or you may visit their Facebook, Twitter, Instagram, or LinkedIn page? What happens if the company or the person doesn't appear in the search engine results? What is your first impression about a friend or a co-worker when you can't find them online in this digital age?

Having a presence in social media is of immense significance, it will help you:

1. Improve your visibility...

If your visibility is confined to the premises of your organization, or industry at best after 5 years of hard work, then realize that you are doing something wrong. You can easily increase your visibility in a short span of time if you are active on social media. Besides working hard, you also need to work smart to ensure that you don't deplete yourself while no one knows about what you are doing. Remember, what gets seen gets sold, and this statement is true for products and people!

2. Build your personal and professional brand…

We always hear about commercial brands, but did you know that every individual is also a brand? Your personal brand is what you bring in as a unique individual, your identity. Your professional brand is how you represent yourself to your colleagues and customers. Especially in this age of technology and social media, you need to seriously think about what you stand for and how to distinguish yourself from the many others out there in the market. It's very similar to what drives people to choose a specific brand over another; the features and the benefits. Apply the same on your brand, focusing more on the benefits. Ask yourself, what value am I adding? What problems can I solve uniquely? And which channels will help me be more available to my peers and customers?

3. Reach a bigger audience in less time and money…

We are living in a golden age when it comes to information and communication, and I personally have a problem with people who still whine and complain. Imagine how much time and money our predecessors used to spend on traditional advertising or traveling to be seen and known by others. Now, we are blessed to have all this available at the click of a button. We can reach a bigger audience with minimum time, money, and efforts. We have all these social media channels available as apps on our smartphones. It's up to us to utilize these to highlight our work and boost our careers.

4. Enjoy two-way communication…

One of the most pragmatic benefits of using social media compared to other mediums is that it allows you to facilitate two-way instant communication between you and your audience. It enables you to interact in real time, get immediate feedback and instantly feel the pulse of your audience or followers, then provides them with what they are looking for in your upcoming posts.

5. Get to know what's happening in your field, industry, and community…

Being present in key social media channels enables you to stay connected and remain up to date with what's going on in your industry, profession, and community. If you follow your company's social media channels you will receive regular notifications of the latest news and promotions, there. I follow major professional organizations' pages like those of CIPD, PMI, CTI, etc. and occasionally participate in their virtual communities, and hence I know about the new trends in HR, the latest templates in project management as well as imminent networking events for coaches.

★★★

According to Brandwatch.com; the world's leading social intelligence company, here are some amazing social media facts and statistics:

- As of October 2017, the internet has 3.5 billion users and there are 3.03 billion active social media users.
- Social media users grew by 121 million between Q2 2017 and Q3 2017, which translates into one new social media user every 15 seconds.
- Facebook adds 500,000 new users every day; that's 6 new profiles every second.
- 500 million people visit Twitter each month without logging in.
- There are 800 million Monthly Active Users on Instagram who upload over 95 million photos each day.
- LinkedIn, the popular professional network platform has 500 million members and 106 million of those, access the site on a monthly basis.

Think of the endless possibilities that you may miss if the right people and companies aren't able to notice your talents and great contributions because of your minimum visibility in such platforms. Moreover, imagine how many years of extra work you'd need to put in to achieve the same level of success without being present in social media. If you decide to ignore utilizing social media at a time when it is believed to be the secret weapon of the 21st century, let me assure you that you are slowing down your pace towards the attainment of your goals. You should understand that success doesn't just come to those who work hard, it also comes to those who work smart. Therefore, employing social media capabilities in a smart way can accelerate your journey towards career success.

Celebrating UAE National Day 2017 in Jumeirah Zabeel Saray Hotel

Overlooking the role that online marketing and social media have on building and boosting your brand can have detrimental effects on your career success. More so for a hotelier.

If you are willingly or unwillingly choosing not to make effective use of these platforms to showcase your best work and contributions to your field, then you are wasting your time and efforts, and will continue remaining in the background. Capitalizing on social media in the right manner is undoubtfully your passport to land your next career break, business venture or speaking engagement.

Even though everyone uses social media channels, very few professionals leverage social media to showcase their work and take their career to the next level. Some of their concerns may include:

O1 *What if my employer sets restrictions on what employees can post and share on social media channels?*

R1 As you know, every coin has two sides and social media is no different. There are some general guidelines and commonly accepted norms on the usage of social media that you need to keep in mind. As long as you don't violate any agreements, breach confidentiality or invade someone's personal space, you are good to post and take advantage of the various social media platforms. These days, there is an attitude of encouraging organizations to involve their employees and partner with them to build the company's employer brand.

There are lots of campaigns running to educate companies to empower their employees to share useful content and inspiring stories; the latest one I encountered was LinkedIn Elevate, a tool that was launched by LinkedIn for this purpose. However, keep in mind, it's ultimately about you and how you position yourself personally and professionally. Yet, if you manage to kill two birds with one stone i.e. benefit yourself as well as your employer with positive exposure using social media, then what can be better than that? You may check with the marketing communication or brand strategy department in your organization to understand the do's and don'ts there, however, from my personal experience, companies would usually welcome any positive word of mouth or free marketing that will expand their reach and promote them to potential employees, customers, and investors.

O2 *What if I'm keen on using social media to build my brand but don't know where to start?*

R2 As mentioned earlier, first, start by familiarizing yourself with the common practices and be aware of what to avoid. You may also want to look at different profiles on various social media channels to benchmark and get more ideas and clarity. I recommend that you start as an observer and notice what the key influencers are doing. Be authentic in your posts and interactions and don't attempt to copy someone else. Focus on posting quality content because you may have heard that content is king. Your main intention should be sharing experiences and enriching lives. If you do this consistently long enough, you will gain the trust of others and expand your network as a result. This was how I did it. No rocket science, just common sense. Of course, like any other thing, you will keep on adding to your learnings and getting better the more you do of it. The feedback you receive from your audience will be a good indicator whether you are on track. Thank those who take the time and efforts to read your posts and reciprocate.

Overall, you need to be mindful of the fact that everything you post online impacts your personal brand and professional reputation. Simply ask yourself… How do I want to be known?

O3 *To what extent is it acceptable to share my personal posts and photos on social media platforms?*

R3 Good question. It's always worth remembering that having good balance and judgment will enable you to make the right decision about what to post, where to post and how often. The main intent must be building your brand, not compromising your privacy online. There are a few factors to consider in this regard. First, note which platform you are using; is it a social network like Facebook, twitter or Instagram or professional networks like LinkedIn or Opportunity. The tone needs to change according to the type of the medium you are posting in to appeal to your audience. For example, you won't go and post a photo of your dinner meal on LinkedIn, but you would easily do so on your Instagram or Facebook.

Secondly, it's important that you show the humane aspect. In other words, while you won't necessarily post a picture of your dinner meal on LinkedIn, which is a professional network, you wouldn't want to miss the opportunity of posting a picture with your team having dinner, during a team outing while leaving a "Thank you" note for them or talking about the importance of having happy and engaged employees at work. Just use your judgment on different circumstances and think about the main intent of initially having your profile created on all these platforms. Another note on this point; people will be better able to relate to you if you show them different aspects of your life. If you constantly talk only about work, office, and projects; you will sound monotonous and robotic. There is no harm in occasionally sharing about an interesting place you have visited or something meaningful you have experienced with your family or on your own. The bottom line; make your posts balanced yet alive.

How do you do that? Here are three simple steps for you to get started:

1. Keep your bio and display pictures updated in all your key social media accounts.

We have discussed earlier in this chapter how your presence in social media channels will promote your visibility as a hotelier and help you establish your personal and professional brand. In order to create a positive emotional connection with your audience and followers, you will need to maintain a concrete profile page in platforms like Facebook, Twitter and Instagram and have a presentable profile picture. Your profile page need to reflect your identity, calling and unique selling points. Your efforts will be in vain if your bio is not up to the mark. With LinkedIn being a professional network, you need to be even more intact. Your LinkedIn profile must be up to date showcasing your best work and achievements. I remember my early beginnings with social media. I'd created profiles in several channels but was not using them much.

With time, I was not getting any value out of those platforms and therefore had a period of time when I stopped posting. It was just about four years ago that I defined a social media strategy and which channels to focus on and how often I'm going to post. I decided to focus on Facebook, Twitter, Instagram, and LinkedIn. So, I started with creating my bio and adding a good profile picture in those channels. I planned the frequency of posts and stuck to my plan and started seeing the difference in a short while. The traffic to my profiles and the number of likes and comments I was receiving increased compared to the time before I had polished my bio and had a picture.

This told my audience a lot about my attitude and helped me build trust and create more followers.

2. Post quality content and increase the level of interaction with your audience.

After taking care of your profile page, start thinking about what you will be posting, how often and on which platform. You've also got to consider your after-post activities, interact with your audience, add value, and contribute; thank those who like or comment on your posts and reciprocate, refrain from having lame discussions and project a professional image all the time.

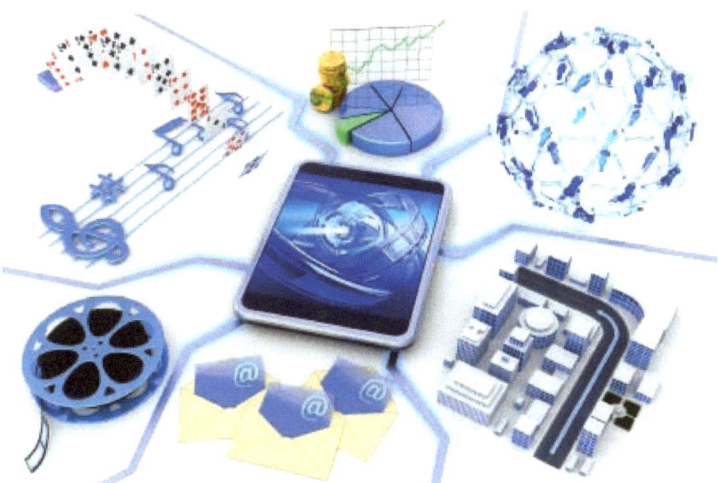

Besides, keep on getting creative about how to interact with your audience. According to an article published in the American Express Business Forum; the most notable social media trends have been and will always remain "interactive media." This means individuals and businesses who don't provide interactive elements like audio, videos, animation, and surveys through their social media accounts will need to catch up to stay current. You don't necessarily need to hire social media developers or invest big amounts to manage your various social media channels, you can easily have a plan and stick to it to remain in touch with your audience. Most of the channels have live streaming capability these days, moreover, creating short useful videos to deliver specific messages are not difficult to do. In fact, you can occasionally include a survey, like in twitter and sense check the inclinations of your followers and what they would like you to talk or tweet about. This makes it more interactive and helps you focus purely on what your audience is asking you to post or present for them.

3. Consider the 50/50 rule for personal effectiveness.

Anything worthwhile in this life takes time to build, and positive social media reputation is no different. You've got to be very disciplined about posting quality content regularly and sharing your best work and talents to be considered a value adding contributor and influencer by other people. In fact, around 50% of your time must be invested in building your personal and professional brand, and in my view, that's the best use of your time. Showing up in your office, hitting the ground running and achieving your key performance indicators and targets are all great things, but that's only half of your duty. What are you doing to build an outstanding personal and professional brand and increase your exposure to become a powerful and irreplaceable force in your industry and profession? How are you taking advantage of all the existing resources and technology to stand out and build a better future for yourself and others?

Most people are neglecting the other 50% of what they are supposed to do and that's why they will always be at the mercy of someone else's decisions or the marketplace conditions. It makes me really sad when I see passionate hoteliers putting years of hard work into their jobs, and then getting back nothing equivalent to it or being unable to move ahead in their careers simply because they didn't take the time to do the most necessary work of building their personal and professional brand over those years.

I myself have benefited big time once I started opening up and sharing my knowledge, experiences and accomplishments on social media to various audiences. This helped me become visible and my work to be known to other people. If no one knows who you are, what you stand for and the value you are adding after so many years of constantly working hard, then you are doing something seriously wrong! Get up, develop an effective strategy to leverage on social media and start working on the 50% that you have been ignoring till now.

3 Actions you should take as a result of reading this chapter:

1. Choose 2 platforms, one is social network i.e. Facebook or Instagram, another is professional network i.e. LinkedIn. Create an account if you don't have one already. If you do, ensure you have an updated bio and display picture. You may have a look at other profiles to get some idea.

2. Start off with your social networks and have one post every alternate day. Make it a post that'll add value to other people's lives. As for LinkedIn, you may leave a comment on an existing post that has interested you or have your own post and make it relevant to your field. In LinkedIn, one to two posts or comments a week will be sufficient.

3. Make it interactive, as this is the whole point of being there. Whether someone comments on your post or replies to your comment, acknowledge their contributions, and share your point of view. If you become consistent with this, people will appreciate your professionalism, and join your network which will in turn build your positive reputation online.

Suggested reading for this chapter:

Seth Price and Barry Feldman assert in their book "The Road to Recognition" that you own a brand, and this brand is your own name. It's up to you to take ownership of it and build it to earn recognition as an expert in your field. They also provide actionable advice for developing your personal brand and accelerating your professional success and share insights from professionals who are reaping the rewards of recognition.

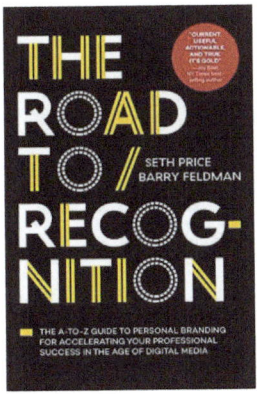

"If you are not online, you don't exist."
~ **Peter Cochrane**

9
Expand Your Network

"If you want to go fast, go alone, if you want to go far go with others."
~ **African Proverb**

Have you ever wondered what is the one thing to cultivate exhaustively throughout the span of your life, which will end up providing you with great privileges and some of the most rewarding life opportunities and thus, make your life easier? It's your network of social and professional contacts whom you have established on the basis of mutual wellbeing and who will be willing to support you in your success journey. Would you like to know how? Here are some of the benefits of expanding your network:

1. Boost your profile...

The best way to be well-known on a wider scale is to keep attending as many events as you can to get noticed by as many people as possible. The more you get seen in such events, the more your face will become familiar to other people. A huge part of succeeding is simply showing up, so by being in the right places at the right times, you'll increase your chances of meeting the right people.

2. Open new doors and opportunities...

Provided you develop the ability to showcase your unique talents and skills; knowing the right people can open new doors of opportunities to you and expose you to some

A Photo with A Former Colleague Nafla Nabhan and The HR Guru Dave Ulrich in 2015

rewarding life experiences that will give your career extra leverage and flavor. Personally, my interactions with new people in networking events unlocked a lot of doors and possibilities which I was unaware of beforehand.

3. Facilitate the exchange of information and ideas...

Meeting new people will also facilitate the constant flow of new information as well as ideas that will help all involved to stay aware and well-informed. Besides, learning from others is regarded as one of the smartest and most time-effective ways to acquire knowledge and develop second hand experience.

4. Increase your chances of helping others...

Helping others can be the most self-fulfilling act you do in your life. In order to help other people, you need to connect with them first. The more people you connect with, the more chances you get to offer help and vice versa; you give other people the opportunity to help you and feel good about themselves as a result. Being in HR for so many years, I strongly believe that your ability to connect with others will determine your success or failure. You can connect with people through your open body language, by lending them a listening ear and making a genuine effort to help in any way you can. Let me also highlight that people generally value the time you invest to listen to them and provide them with potential solutions from your experiences. That is a great way to build trust and strengthen your relationships with others.

5. Extend your support network...

Whether it's the next speaking engagement, award recommendation, or simply the next career break, you can get any or all of these with minimum or no hassle when you know someone everywhere. Your immediate contacts will be very much willing to help you in your success journey and be a part of your story. Every person in your network potentially knows other people directly or indirectly who can be of help to you and the same is true for you. After all, networking is all about being able to uplift each other in comradery and celebrate each other's accomplishments.

★★★

A recent study by Right Management found for the fifth year in a row, that person-to-person networking is the most effective way of finding a new job. Networking had a 46 percent effectiveness rate, compared to Internet job boards (25 percent), recruiters (14 percent), the direct approach (7 percent) and newspaper listings (1 percent).

Are you still curious how this is applicable to the hotel industry? Especially here in the Middle East, where most businesses operate on relationships, we hoteliers, should be the first people to go out there and tell the world about what we do and the beauty of our industry.

During My Interaction with H.H Sheikh Maktoum Bin Mohammed Al Maktoum in Careers UAE 2014

Perhaps that's why many people don't know much about the details of our work in hotels and how we contribute. According to my personal experience, working in hotels is one of the most interesting careers, still, it's the least represented in social and professional networking events because most of us are not willing to step out of our own hotels and industry boundaries and mingle with people from other sectors.

If you don't take the time to build and foster meaningful alliances during your working life, don't wonder why it's taking you double the time and efforts to get in your life what your well-connected colleague or friend managed to achieve within half of that time and lesser effort. Imagine how frustrating it can be to miss on valuable opportunities to showcase your talent, talk about your contributions or share your expertise in front of the movers and shakers in high-profile business conferences in your city just because you don't know the organizers or someone within the network to grant you a speaking opportunity there.

During Business Breakfast with My Colleague Dinesh Chaudhari and Dr. Marshall Goldsmith in 2015

Guess what such an opportunity could have done to your career and growth! You must spend your time on something. Either invest it in nurturing worthwhile relationships that will expose you to potential advancement opportunities or divest it in unnecessary duplication of efforts in the hope that you will be noticed one day and get what you deserve. The decision is yours!

Working in travel, tourism and hospitality provide employees with unique opportunities to meet and interact with people from different walks of life. Think of the various occupations i.e. doctors, entrepreneurs or motivational speakers; educational levels i.e. PhD holders, professors or thought leaders; social and economic classes i.e. ministers or presidents whom you will come across over the course of your career in this industry.

During Jumeirah Creekside Hotel's Annual Staff Party 2017 with Dubai Duty Free Vice Chairman and CEO Colm McLoughlin

You just need to be smart about how to utilize such opportunities and create mutually beneficial relationships for both parties. That's the main reason why God didn't give us everything, so that we benefit one another, exchange knowledge, and help each other. After all, your network is the people who want to help you, and you want to help them, and that's really powerful as rightly indicated by Reid Hoffman.

So, if that was the case, why do we see many working professionals working in silos and not making a lot of efforts to expand their network and build mutually beneficial relationships? Let's examine some of the underlying concerns that they might have:

O1 *Are you trying to say that my talents and capabilities will not help me much to grow and succeed if I don't know the right people?*

1. Your Networks & Relationships
- Your Vertical & Horizontal Networks

2. Your Talents & Skills
- Focus On Your Strengths

3. Your Life Experiences
- Your Unique Expertise & Wisdom

Success Trilogy

R1 Again, this is one of those things that is not either/or. Success comes to people who choose balance in key life aspects. There is no doubt that your strengths when constantly polished and employed in the right manner will become your talents which will give you an edge in what you do. Meanwhile, this in no way contradicts with building and nurturing your network.

Let me introduce you to something called "The Success Trilogy" here. This is a combination of the 3 things that will help you achieve tremendous success and grow your income in an excellent way.

1. The first element is your network and relationships. Throughout the span of your career, you need to make an effort to expand your relationships vertically and horizontally. An example of a vertical relationship is someone in a more powerful position than you, like a CEO of a major corporation, a diplomat or a president of state or country. Whereas your horizontal network includes people who are in the same level in your field or profession as well as those contacts who are in the same rank as you from different sectors. To clarify, as I am a Director of HR in the hotel industry, my vertical network will be VP's, C-Suite level executives, media personalities and influencers, state ministers and presidents. While my horizontal network will be hoteliers and HR professionals in other sectors. In fact, this can also include other people from other professions like finance, IT etc. People from other fields but at the same level.

2. The second element is your talents and skills. As highlighted in the last part of chapter 2, you can start by taking Clifton Strength Finder Assessment to identify your key strengths. Once you've done that, you need to refine those strengths to turn them into unique talents and supplement them with the required skills. An example of this is if your talent is writing, then besides polishing it by consistent practice, you are also required to learn some additional skills that will help you showcase this talent to the world and spread your message on a wider scale. These skills include but are not limited to public speaking, marketing, negotiating, blogging, networking, etc.

3. The third element is your unique experiences that will present you as a specialist and expert in your field. It saves you time, as you will likely know the nuts and the bolts of your industry and profession, and thus increase your self-worth, which will ultimately influence your net worth in a positive way. Your life experiences are one of your most unique assets that you can capitalize on in the long-term.

In general, you need to work on developing all the 3 elements of this success trilogy simultaneously throughout your life, to become very effective in your life and build a competitive edge. However, in this chapter we will just focus on the relationship aspect.

Q2 *What if I have a good presence online across different social media channels? I have also built a big network on*

LinkedIn. Do I still need to attend events and meet people face to face?

R2 Good question. Where do you think you will build trust faster, online, or offline? No one can deny the importance of having online visibility these days both for individuals and companies, yet, networking online is only half the job done. Human interaction surpasses any kind of online marketing or social media.

Look at the majority of those reputed organizations that we know, despite them investing considerable amounts on online brand building initiatives, they still have a dedicated team of sales and marketing professionals who attend road shows, and trade exhibitions to meet potential clients, earn their trust and build mutually fruitful relationships for the clients and the business. The same concept applies to individuals; no matter how tech savvy we become, we still need the human element to interact with people and build long-lasting relationships based on trust. As we said earlier, maintain balance in all aspects of your life to achieve success.

Q3 *Would it help to distribute as many business cards as possible when I attend networking events?*

R3 Many people confuse networking with distributing business cards. You don't build relationships by passing on as many business cards to as many people during a networking event. Your focus must be on individuals and having meaningful conversations with them. Also look for balance in a way that you can talk about yourself and give other people the chance to tell you something interesting about them; so, you are creating a win-win situation for both. In most cases, you need to be willing to offer your services for free before you expect to receive something in return. This is an important stepping stone and investment towards building trust-based relationships and thus accelerating your career success.

So, once we have explored the common concerns professionals may have about networking, let's provide you with some tips and tools to help you start building personally and professionally meaningful relationships to boost your career:

1. You need to consistently have the right intentions, and turn them into effective actions keeping faith that you will slowly but surely reap what you sow.

I can't help but give the analogy of the Chinese Bamboo Trees; wherein the farmers who cultivate Chinese Bamboo Trees don't see any evidence of life for the plants in the first five years! Regardless, they need to continue watering them every single day and keeping faith that one day their bamboo trees will rise high and provide for their future generations. Similarly, building networks and nurturing them takes time until they start yielding the benefits. You need to keep nurturing them for a while and look at them as potential investments for your future.

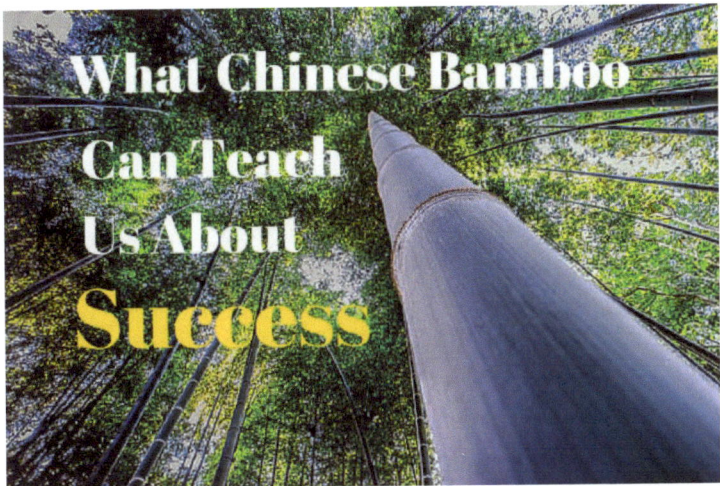

I was very impressed with one lady in my network when she was talking about how she started attending networking events. Her story is quite interesting. She says that after she realized the importance of networking, she made up her mind to attend at least two networking events every week! (That's quite a stretch, even for me)! She says despite how challenging it was for her to commit to this, she still did it knowing that the long-term benefits for her professional and business growth would be tremendous. Some days, those events were scheduled early in the mornings and she really had to push herself to wake up to purely go and expand her network. The outcome? After 5 years of consistent efforts, she was able to expand her reach, author 7 books and build a successful 7 figure business in Australia. She had even entered new markets like the US and Middle East. This is all of course as a result of her hard work, but also her continuous efforts to meet a lot of interesting people from different walks of life and countries, that helped her get the opportunities she needed to spread her message and build her presence in the marketplace and establish her unique brand. This is none other than the amazing lady; Natasa Denman. Her life motto is "Take Action, No Excuses and Focus on Goals."

2. Attend key online and offline networking events that are relevant to your industry, profession, and personal interests.

Online networking events include but are not limited to online conference calls, webinars, blogs, discussion forums, etc. Examples of offline networking events

Moderating A Panel Discussion During MICE Quotient's LEAD Symposium 2017 in Dubai

include conferences, seminars, workshops, career fairs and all kinds of social and professional meetups in which you can meet and interact with people face-to-face. Your plan should be to maintain a balance between attending both online and offline networking events.

Ask yourself: "In which events and forums will I be able to meet potential people with whom can I collaborate and further personal and professional goals?" – then simply attend those events with a clear purpose.

A few years back, I had a vision of establishing myself as a renowned Emirati Hospitality Professional, so I started searching for all the relevant events i.e. conferences, exhibitions, awards, etc. then making time to attend some of them. This has proved to be a great step for me towards achieving my vision. You really need to get out there and be frequently seen in such events to become the face of your industry and profession.

3. Do more speaking Gigs either by applying, requesting, or simply getting recommended.

This is one of the best ways to share your expertise, boost your credibility and meet new people as a result. You can apply for speaking engagements, request the organizers if you know them, or ask someone in your network to recommend you if they know the organizers.

I'll tell you how I got my first speaking opportunity. I have a habit of attending several networking events in a year (not as much as I'd like to though), especially the key industry or profession related events. One of these key events in UAE is The Hotel Show. I heard about this event for the first time in 2013 and got curious about it. It's a very interesting platform that brings everything related to hospitality under one roof. So, in 2013, I participated as a recruiter on my day off. My name and contact details were on the main manual. I got a good idea about the event and met some interesting people.

Since then I've made sure to attend every edition of it even if I go as a visitor. After 3 years of consistently attending the hotel show, the organizers reached out to me to take part in a panel discussion! I was very delighted with this opportunity and went for it. It was a very rewarding experience to share the stage with some of the most reputed industry professionals to talk about *"Creating Sustainable Hospitality Assets."*

This session was a big success and gave me a lot of exposure. People were very engaged and asked a lot of interesting questions. This panel discussion was then captured in the next Edition of Hotelier Middle East Magazine (October 2016).

From my end, I ensured to share my experience and capitalize on this exposure in my social media channels where people showed more interest and further interacted by either following me or commenting on my posts. Within only one week of this, I received another invitation to speak during MENA HR Summit in Abu Dhabi about "Happiness in the Workplace!"

Speaking About Happiness in the Workplace During MENA HR Summit 2016

The bottom line here? It's true that success breeds success, however, in order to create such possibilities in your life and career, you need to consciously have a clear direction for your life and supplement it by employing the right tools and techniques. The network that you build throughout your life is one of your key assets and a great stepping stone to your next exciting break.

3 Actions you should take as a result of reading this chapter:

1. Identify the right networking opportunities for you based on your industry, profession, and interests. Start attending no less than two networking events per month until you become more comfortable. Focus on quality rather than quantity. Use websites like Eventbrite.com and meetup.com to locate relevant events near you. Networking events don't have to be dull and serious. In fact, you won't get much out of attending them if you don't enjoy yourself. You can even start by joining a nearby meet up to learn a new language or cooking or developing a mobile app! The objective here is to meet as many new people as possible.

2. Based on the first element of Success Trilogy discussed earlier in this chapter; make a list of all the horizontal and vertical relationships that you have cultivated till now in your career. Now, look at the short and long-term life goals that you have set for yourself in chapter 3 (Design Your Future), and identify which relationship will help you further your goals. Ask yourself the following questions:

- Which existing relationships do I need to nurture more? How can I do that?
- Which new relationships do I need to build? How can I do that?
- By when do I need to do this?

Once you've got your answers, put a six months action plan, and take responsibility to act on it. Review your action plan monthly to measure your progress and re-align accordingly.

3. Stay informed about the key conferences, seminars and workshops that will be attended by key influencers and peers in your profession or industry and make an effort to attend to connect with like-minded people. Keep in mind that not all these conferences, seminars and workshops are necessarily paid events. I've personally attended many high-quality events which were free of charge but helped me to meet new people and build my professional network.

Suggested reading for this chapter:

In his bestselling book "Emotional Intelligence", Daniel Goleman delineates the five crucial skills of emotional intelligence, and shows how they determine our success in relationships, work, and even our physical well-being. Emotionally intelligent people are smart about building better relationships with themselves and others and thus more likely to succeed in their lives.

"The richest people in the world look for and build networks, everyone else looks for work."

~ Robert Kiyosaki

10
Snatch the Spotlight

"Vulnerability is not about winning, and it's not about losing. It's about having the courage to show up and be seen."
~ **Brene Brown**

Participating and winning in industry and professional awards can give you and your organization a competitive edge. From my personal experience, I've noticed that most individuals and companies are reluctant to participate in such awards events and be highlighted. This is mainly due to their perception that this is too self-promotional as well as the process of writing and submitting an award-entry is very time consuming (ask me)! Nevertheless, I believe the benefits of doing so outweigh all the reasons not to, as follows:

1. Self-exposure to wider audiences...

This is unlike the limited reach of company specific recognition schemes, which is only confined within the boundaries of your organization. Participation in industry awards provides you broad exposure in front of your industry, as well as professional peers and extends your reach even beyond that, which in turn accelerates your career growth and opens unlimited opportunities for your future.

2. Increase your credibility and chances of promotion...

Once you have been conferred with several reputed awards in a specific industry or field, your name will be more recognizable to the big people in that domain and your face becomes familiar. This builds up your reputation and makes you more credible compared to your colleagues who may be working as hard, but no one outside their own organizations would have heard of them. When opportunities for promotion come up, your chances will be higher to be considered for them.

3. Draw the attention of potential employers...

I have personally experienced this after winning two key accolades in one of the most reputable professional awards. The very next day, I received a call from a leading organization who was also present the previous night and had won in another category. I had a nice chat with that person and explained to him that I appreciate him thinking about me, however, I love the hospitality industry and am not thinking to change sectors any time soon. This is only one scenario besides the potential employers who continue approaching me on LinkedIn after they view my strong profile and awards. Always remember, what gets seen gets sold! This applies to products as well as people.

4. Attract new opportunities to highlight and reward your achievements and contributions...

People like to associate themselves with successful people, because success attracts success, and this also gives them the confidence that they can also do it. There were many occasions where I met some great people during award ceremonies, talked a bit and exchanged contact details. After a while, the same people contacted me to discuss collaboration opportunities or invited me to seminars or workshops to attend or to speak. Your career will get more interesting once it spreads beyond the premises of your company and your contacts extend further than your co-workers. Try it and thank me later.

5. Elevate your status, self-esteem and worth...

It's an amazing feeling to be recognized in front of a big audience for your efforts and hard work. This boosts your self-confidence, raises your status, and increases your value in the job market. Beware, as this can become truly addictive after some time; again, try to find the balance in everything you do in life to be sustainable.

★★★

From my own humble experience of participating in award events over the years, I've noticed that hospitality companies have very little to no representation in such events. Of course, specific industry awards like Hotelier Middle East Awards, The Hotel Show Awards, and Hospitality Excellence Awards (to name a few), are anyway dedicated to hotel and travel sectors, so you will naturally see them there. The interesting thing though, you will see the same people participating or attending these events every year.

All Winners in Hozpitality Excellence Awards 2015

On another note, hoteliers' participation in other professional awards like Finance, Human Resources, IT, Leadership, etc. is very limited. When I participate in professional awards say HR or Leadership because they are relevant to what I do, I am unable to locate a single hospitality professional or company there. In fact, most participants are from banks, healthcare, or government institutions. I just don't understand why hoteliers are so hesitant to highlight their valuable contributions to the community by attending such events to network and be visible to other sectors.

So why is it a good idea to participate in and win industry awards? What could possibly happen if you don't? Let's take real life examples from what we see in our circles as hoteliers. Imagine spending all your career working and working and working, yet when you resign or retire (that is if you were not made redundant), your chapter ends there, and all those great guest comments that you have received or the several high-end projects that you have completed stay confined within the premises of your ex-hotel, then get forgotten with time!

Jumeirah Creekside Hotel HR Team named HR Team of the Year During MENA HR Excellence Awards 2016

Think of all the sleepless nights when you did night duty and compromised your health and all the parent-teacher meetings that you had to miss and upset your kid because you had to be present for an important VIP event that your hotel was hosting. You may be selected for "Colleague of the Month Award", an internal recognition scheme in your hotel if you were lucky enough to fit the criteria and be supported by your manager, but what if you don't? Besides, ask yourself, is the purpose of your hospitality career to be known only within the premises of your company? What will be your token of appreciation and badge of honor to talk about and show to your grandchildren 20, 30 or 40 years from now? Think about it.

Hoteliers will undoubtedly get extensive value out of participating in and winning relevant industry and profession related awards and accolades. Especially here in the Middle East, where we have some of the most captivating hotels with state of the art facilities and luxury services. Hoteliers are constantly required to exert extra efforts to deliver exemplary guest experiences and exceed expectations. In the midst of such busy operations and the pursuit to fulfil others' expectations, you, the gatekeeper of such excellent calling, regardless of your role or department, would mostly go unnoticed, unless either - 1) Someone notices and recognizes you or 2) You yourself take the time to talk about your own contributions by nominating yourself for and winning those awards. In your opinion, which one has more value for your hotel career and is much more empowering for you as an individual?

Awards recognize your talents and contributions that help you stand out among your peers. The hospitality industry is already full of style and glamour, so hoteliers should be amongst the first to embrace this lifestyle and be in the limelight themselves, rather than just working from behind the scenes to facilitate such events for others and acting as passive observers.

Despite all these benefits and extensive visibility that can be gained, I see a lot of professionals and specifically hoteliers reluctant to claim that well deserved recognition! Following are three common objections that I usually hear from people when I discuss the importance of participating in industry and professional awards with them:

O1 *What if my employer doesn't allow me to participate in external award events?*

R1 I see no reason why this would be the case. Yes, I've heard certain people saying such things either because they are not sure or as a good excuse for not doing it. In general, people are very nice and if you ask them for recommendations and testimonials to support your award submission, they wouldn't mind, provided they see the value you are adding in your field of work. Besides, if your company or manager sees your willingness to participate, they are going to cheer you up and even guide you through the process. The point here is that you need to take ownership and follow through during the submission process to ensure you have fulfilled all the submission requirements. In a worst-case scenario, where you don't see your employer being supportive, you can still enter the awards by writing the award entry yourself and asking your trusted co-workers to recommend you.

It's great if your company supports your entry and helps you with the submission, however, keep in mind it's not the only way. You can also do it yourself unless the respective award criteria say otherwise. I know from my personal experience of entering various awards that you can write the entry and submit it yourself. Just don't use your employer as an excuse for putting your career growth on hold!

Q2 *If applying for industry awards and winning them is such a lucrative experience, why would many hoteliers shy away from doing that?*

R2 Great question! I've always wondered about this and initially couldn't comprehend it but now after so many years, I know the answer. Firstly, it's all the attention that the person gets when he/she enters into such awards. Many people are not very comfortable being in the

Winning the HR Professional of the Year Award During the MENA HR Excellence Awards 2016

limelight and prefer to be in the background. Now call it fear, low self-confidence or laziness. It's not everyone's cup of tea. This is just what it is. Secondly, people generally hesitate to be named the best, the first or the most influential, because once they get such titles they feel happy at that point, however, that means they need to continuously put much more efforts to maintain such titles or self-image to not lose credibility. In other words, they are afraid of commitment to excellence because it can be very demanding.

Although, in human nature, once a person gets that kind of recognition, they will feel obliged to fulfil their responsibility towards other people and be compelled to thrive and deliver excellence even in the most challenging circumstances. Besides, the feeling of winning can be very addictive (Ask me)! The third reason I realized from my own experience is that writing award entries can be very time and energy consuming, and most people don't see the value of putting all that effort while they are unable to guarantee their win. If you have never taken part in such awards, you won't have any idea about how they work.

This is not something that you will learn in a hotel school or business college. This is plain life experience that took me many years of hard work, trial, and error to acquire and figure out, which now you can benefit from. Be sure to make use of it!

Q3 *I feel I deserve to be awarded for my great work. What if everyone in my company is too busy to notice that and recognize me?*

R3 This is a common scenario which I've personally undergone during a certain stage in my hospitality career. Initially it led me towards terrible disappointment and self-pity because I knew the quality of my deliverables, and the immense efforts I had to put in to turn those abstract business concepts into effective results. Yet, I wondered, why no one was impressed or talked loudly about my outstanding work!? I'm thankful that that painful experience helped me grow, mature, and find better alternatives to get recognized and showcase my excellent work. It liberated me to take charge and get exposure on a larger scale. And this is exactly what you also must do.

You need to realize that everyone around you is really busy and self-absorbed. Even if they may have the best intentions, they themselves may not know how to do it, so you better take responsibility and go figure it out yourself.

*Named Judges Choice HR Director of the Year
During Hozpitality Excellence Awards 2015*

You owe it to your career and to all the hard work that you have been doing ever since you got into the world of hospitality. First, go back to chapter 3 of this book; (Design Your Life) to understand that you and only you are the one responsible for your life and happiness. As Joel Osteen says: *"Don't just accept whatever comes your way in life. You were born to win; you were born for greatness; you were created to be a champion in life."* Then have a glance at chapter 6 of this book; (Surprise Your Employer) and incorporate the principles mentioned there in your work to deliver excellence and have multiple evidences of your contributions and how you have consistently added value or solved business problems.

Don't just sit, wait, and whine about the fact that no one notices your amazing work and that you don't get recognized as often as you should be. You know the method as well as have the tools now, get up and make it happen. There is no point in begging people to recognize you; that's pathetic. The best alternative is, let them celebrate you, now that's a powerful and more attractive position to be in.

Now, let me provide you with three tips to help you start participating in and winning awards that will distinguish you and recognize your valuable contributions to your field of work:

1. Look for the prominent awards and accolades in your industry and profession and plan to participate in two to three of them every year.

Jumeirah Creekside HR director lauded for her work

Nikhil Pereira, *October 29th, 2015*

The director of human resources at the Jumeirah Creekside Hotel Dubai Mona Abdulla AlHebsi, won the HR & Training Person of the Year Award at the Hotelier Middle East Awards 2015.

AlHebsi began her career as a fresher in the hospitality industry back in 2003, steadily working her way up the ranks until 2008; where she swapped hospitality for education. After spending four years in Zayed University AlHebsi returned to the industry, eventually reuniting with her former bosses – Jumeirah in 2014.

At her role she has gained plenty of accolades for the various training and development methods and tools she has implemented.

AlHebsi has been responsible for organising various activities for all departments on a regular basis to ensure they are engaged and having fun while going about routine tasks.

Some of these activities include: team building activities, constant recognition of employee efforts and launching the employee initiative, monthly audio books and learning discussion sessions, exposure to senior management in the hotel, team meals and get-togethers, talks from external speakers on a monthly basis on various topics and providing support to balance the integration of work and personal life.

"In 2005, when I started out in Jumeirah, I was part of the first batch of Emirati ladies to work in hospitality, having studied over here. Ever since the interest of UAE locals in the field ahs grown tremendously. I feel proud to walk into hotels and see so many cultures and nationalities working together," said AlHebsi on the night, after the award was presented.

AlHebsi is highly educated and is holder of two separate MBA degrees, she also completed several courses in human resources management, training, learning and development.

In addition she has also received several certifications from DTCM and local educational institutions for her contributions to Emiratisation in the hospitality sector and coaching young UAE nationals.

The award was presented by sponsor Emirates Academy of Hospitality Management's director of industry liaison Marianne Saulwick, at the James-Bond themed event which took place at the InterContinental Dubai Festival City.

The shortlisted nominees for this category included InterContinental Jeddah's Anjum Rahim Khan, InterContinental Regency Hotel Bahrain's Maria Corazon Beleno Aguillon, InterContinental Muscat's Salim Al Khatri, Holiday Inn Muscat Al Seeb's Samiya Al Balushi, Radisson Blu Royal Suite Hotel Jeddah's Seymor Ridon.

Don't tell me it's a lot of additional work and you can do without it. Yes, you can sure do without it if you want to spend the next 5, 10 years in the same position with the same salary, doing the same mundane work, while no one knows much about you. You've got to do this if you want to take your career to the next level. Check out the most popular hospitality awards (I've listed them at the end of this chapter), read carefully through the criteria, scan through the categories, select which one is most appropriate for you and if you have sufficient evidences and examples to construct a strong entry, write the entry and submit it before the deadline.

Named 100 Most Influential Global HR Professionals 2016 in Mumbai

Most organizations or individuals who participate in award programs, deal with consultants and award writing agencies to compile and polish their award entries for a fee. It's always a good idea to leave the work for the experts. However, in my case, I'm blessed to have excellent writing skills which I consider my golden coins (see chapter 12), so I enjoy doing this myself. It does take me a lot of time and effort to put together a winning entry, but that's nothing compared to the rewards I gain later as a result of dedicating the time and effort. Remember, the first few years of entering the various awards will be a bit of a pain because you are new to the award committees and judges, and no one knows you. Once you start participating and submitting entries regularly, then you will see things moving in the right direction.

When I started this phase of participating in awards, I didn't leave out any potential award program related to the industry or my field; I searched for and read everything about it thoroughly. I made a long-term plan of participating in two to three awards per year whether I win or not. In fact, after having won so many reputed awards in different domains, I reached a stage in my career now where I don't need to research awards anymore, I simply get recommended or receive invitations to enter by the organizers. Like any other thing in life, this is a status you will earn with time and consistency.

2. Plan your year ahead and construct your success enablers.

As previously mentioned, refer to chapters 3 (Design Your Future) and 6 (Surprise Your Employer) to help yourself with this step. Then, get an idea about the available award programs, their criteria, and categories. Simultaneously, note down your organization's key priorities and the problems in the company that require attention (as mentioned in chapter 6). Further, make a strategy to put them to action and drive initiatives that will bring about improvements in your workplace and positively impact the key performance indicators in business. In addition to your company goals, continue thriving on your personal goals.

This way, as time passes by, you will create great successes to talk about to people and include in your award entry. Once you have a list of achievements, you can go and apply for relevant awards after you customize your submission to fit the respective award criteria.

MENA HR Excellence Awards 2016 Press Release

3. Capitalize on your wins and yield on your loss opportunities.

Consider every participation in an award event as a personal gain and one step that takes you closer to your goals. The more you take part and persevere even if you don't win (and don't expect to win the first few times anyway), just participate for the experience itself. Don't forget, attending glamorous award ceremonies is a great experience by itself. There you can mingle with other people and professionals and expand your network. You can also notice what kind of companies and individuals participate in such events and win. It's good for you to know the best employers and individuals in your industry and field. If you win, well and good, make the most of this win by announcing it in your company through internal communications department, do your own press releases, post on your social media channels, etc.

Hotelier Middle East Awards 2015 Winner's Trophy

In case you don't win, don't feel disheartened, take it as a learning experience and stepping stone that will take you to your next win. For me personally, whenever I didn't win, something else equally good came out of that participation. One good tip I can give you is, if you are looking to win a particular award, and don't win in the first year of application, participate the next year, your chances will be higher. Whether you win or not, what really matters is that you make most of the opportunities available to you during your hotel career and be as active and involved in such external events as you are in your hotel, and to me, that's what signifies a true hotelier.

3 Actions you should take as a result of reading this chapter:

1. Specify your industry and profession. For example, in my case, my industry is Travel, Tourism & Hospitality and my profession is Human Capital or Human Resources. In addition, list down what other awards may be applicable to you based on how you would like to position yourself. In my case, I can easily consider taking part in awards that recognize leadership, coaching or women in business for instance.

2. Once you have done that, search for the most popular awards in your region for those relevant disciplines, let's say the top 3 awards that you will be proud of associating with, and mentioning in your professional profile. Visit the awards website, familiarize yourself with the categories and application process, read through the criteria and evaluate whether you are ready to apply for the next cycle or you require to do more work and gather more evidence to support your entry.

3. It's also worth having a look at the "previous winners" section, especially in the category you are planning to enter in and connect with them to get some useful tips. After my win in one of the awards, I received some queries from a potential applicant who was keen to participate in the same category the following year. That was a very smart decision by them to solicit some useful tips from

a previous winner. This has eventually resulted in them constructing an effective award entry and winning the desired award.

Additional resources for this chapter:

As a hotelier, you must stay informed about your industry's most reputed awards. Ensure to take part in one or many of these prestigious awards during the span of your hotel career. Visit the following websites to learn more:

Logo	Award Name	Website
	Hotelier Middle East Awards	http://www.hoteliermiddleeast.com/awards
	The Hotel Show Awards	https://www.thehotelshow.com/awards/about-the-awards/
	Hozpitality Excellence Awards	http://www.hozpitalityexcelleceawards.com/

"I love winning and any team I'm on, I expect to win."
~ Landon Donovan

Most Influential Woman in Hospitality Human Capital 2017

Jumeirah Group, a member of Dubai Holding, operates a world-class portfolio of luxury hotels, resorts and residences across the Middle East, Europe and Asia. We invited Mona AlHebsi to tell us more about herself, the company and provide advice for those seeking a career in hospitality.

Jumeirah Hotels & Resorts are regarded among the most luxurious and innovative hospitality chains in the world and have won numerous international travel and tourism awards. The company was founded in 1997 with the aim to become a hospitality industry leader through establishing a world class portfolio of luxury hotels and resorts. Mona speaks to us about her career journey in the hospitality industry.

"Throughout a career span of over 12 years, I have worked over 8 years within the hospitality industry. I started a job as Administrative Assistant in the Training Department of Burj Al Arab Jumeirah where I worked for almost three years. After completing my postgraduate studies, I've got an opportunity as HR Manager with Grand Hyatt Dubai. There, I was in charge of establishing the Emiratization strategy of the hotel and managing the day to day HR operation.

"In December 2014, I have returned to Jumeirah, this time as a Director of Human Resources in Jumeirah Creekside Hotel, the contemporary lifestyle brand of Jumeirah. During my time there, I was a member of the Executive Committee in the hotel, heading the HR and Learning and Development division and responsible for designing and implementing effective people strategies in the hotel to support the overall business strategy. I have won several industry awards for my achievements and contributions throughout my tenure with Jumeirah Creekside Hotel." Mona has recently been promoted to Director of Human Resources in the majestic Ottoman inspired resort Jumeirah Zabeel Saray.

Mona urges individuals who would like to be hoteliers to assess their strengths and have a clear picture in mind of what they would like to achieve. The selected job role must be in alignment with their life purpose. She also detailed what attributes are integral to succeed in the industry.

"Like everything else in life, hospitality is not for everyone. To succeed in the hospitality industry, a person should have the flair and the passion to work with different people and make things happen through the combined efforts of a team. Moreover, you must have a strong and yet, a balanced personality. Building your personal brand is a big one, you need to make people aware of your unique selling points; you never know when the next opportunity will be around the corner."

Contact: Mona AlHebsi
Email: mona.alhebsi@jumeirah.com
Address: PO Box 27722, Dubai, UAE
Telephone: +971 4 453 0000
Website: www.jumeirah.com

8 MEA MARKETS / Women in business Awards 2017

11
Dare To Disagree

"The hottest place in hell is reserved for those who remain neutral in times of great moral conflict."
~ **Martin Luther King, Jr**

If you would like to become a person of influence in your life and career, then you need to speak up and have your say in important matters. You won't go very far in your life if your goal is to do just enough to get by and agree to everything being said to you to avoid conflict. This is not to say; go and argue with every other person you are talking to. In fact, the real wisdom is in bypassing the small stuff and staying focused on your main goals. However, there are occasions in life when saying "yes" or remaining quiet is not an option. Here's how being assertive and having your say will bring out positive gains to your life and career:

1. Stay true to your inner values and morals...

Work is a great vehicle to put your core values into practice every single day. It can be a very rewarding experience when the actions you undertake in your job are aligned with your morals. Since your value system is the foundational part of your identity and work is only one piece of it; you shouldn't compromise your values and ethics in the name of your work. Don't let anyone mislead you, there is no flexibility when the matter is about integrity. It's either right or wrong. If saying no at times will make you stay true to your values, then go ahead and do it. There is no bigger loss in life than losing your own conscience.

2. Command respect and authority...

You've got to be very clear about what your role entails. Decide on what you can still be flexible with and what is just unacceptable for you and practice it day in and day out. What makes you unique in the eyes of others are the values on which you operate and your ethical precepts. These are the things that will grant you respect and authority in the early years of your career and continue with you even long after. Don't sell out on them.

3. Define how others talk to you and treat you...

It's human nature that we emanate verbal and non-verbal signals to those around us. This is based on how we consistently talk and act in different situations. People tend to pick up on those signals and form their impressions about us. Those impressions will determine how they deal with us. For instance, if you keep quiet every time your colleagues talk to you disrespectfully, or make a key team decision without involving you, then you are simply asking for more of those scenarios. If such things happen in a work environment, address them directly with the people concerned and clarify your expectations for the future.

4. Increase your influence...

I hope that you are not expecting your professional journey to be a smooth ride without bumps. No matter how hard you try to maintain harmony in the workplace, what you do will always be against someone's best interest, including the right decisions you make. Your patience will be frequently tested, and your success will be determined by your efforts to voice what you see even if some don't want to hear it. Don't expect to make a difference if you can't stand for something. Influential people are called influential for a reason. They are tough cookies who are not easily intimidated by others' authority or status. What matters to them is doing the right things and living a life of integrity and honor.

5. Advance your career...

As you rise through the ranks, you will be involved more frequently in important discussions and big decisions that impact people and business. How you handle those crucial conversations and carry out your role will determine the level of your success. When a suitable assignment presents itself, the senior management in your company will prioritize those people who are visible, fruitfully contribute to key business discussions and have a say in important matters.

★★★

According to 'Decision Wise,' a leading employee engagement firm in the USA, a study was conducted on over 100,000 employees in the USA and they found out that 34% of employees there don't speak up because of the fear of retribution. From my experience, I have been noticing the same trend in most organizations in the UAE. Even though I don't have solid statistics to share, I can well affirm that the percentage in here will be something between 50% and 70% if not more, since most of the workforce is made up of expatriates who come from different parts of the world mainly from the Indian Subcontinent and South East Asia.

Countries in those particular geographical locations are generally characterized to be among the "high-context cultures", which means that the tendency for people coming from those cultural backgrounds is to value long-term relationships with others and obey authority, therefore, they would be more comfortable avoiding conflict, going with the flow, and taking instructions rather than speaking up and challenging the decisions of their superiors.

Unless you develop the courage to define your own voice at work as you mature in your career journey, you will be subject to other people's agendas, and they will keep dictating to you what, how and when to say/do things. If you think keeping quiet during critical situations at work or borrowing other people's voice is the best way to advance, get noticed or win the political game, you are wrong.

Let me highlight something here. In a very recent situation I saw that, when opportunities for promotions, advancements or major projects show up, the very same people for whom you have compromised your own voice and self-respect hoping to please them, will be amongst the first to disqualify you for such advancement opportunities. Because, all you have proved to them till date, is your ability to be a good follower not a good leader, while all the senior roles and the meaningful projects require leaders; people who know how to balance teamwork and business priorities, but not by suppressing their voice or avoiding conflict, when you should be doing the opposite.

As Queen Latifa rightly said: "*It's not always easy to do the right thing. But doing the right thing, makes you strong, it builds your character.*"

Throughout the span of your career, you will be faced with many ethical dilemmas as well as be expected to make decisions or execute high stake matters in your workplace. Whether in hotels, or any other organization, you can't escape this part when you work with people. The majority of the people will be comfortable to stay neutral than to take a stand and assume responsibility for their decisions.

It becomes even more necessary to put your fears aside, speak up and make the right decisions if you are in a leadership position and when you know that keeping quiet in some scenarios will negate your personal values and convictions, impact the lives of other people, and consequently shake your own professional as well as business reputation in the eyes of your key stakeholders.

Even though the benefits of speaking up were explained in this chapter, I know that the majority of professionals will be unwilling to adopt a courageous approach when it comes to discussing major work issues or important career decisions. Reasons? Let's analyze some of these concerns:

O1 *What if speaking up or not supporting a decision that comes from upper management in my company gets me in trouble?*

R1 What if not speaking up got you in trouble? In fact, what if your manager wanted to test the waters to see whether your presence in that position makes any difference?

Even better, what if your employer wanted to test your capability and ethics to decide whether you are a person who can be trusted, and that conclusion will end up driving all future decisions related to your career?

Why does it have to be black or white? If you look in between, you will see all the rainbow colors that give you wider options to choose from, so stop holding onto only one possibility.

Sometimes, you will see practices in the workplace that are against ethics and established conduct, or some individuals who are bullying or sabotaging other people. If you have the authority to stop such practices or reprimand those people, then it's your duty to bring discipline and by doing so you are already having a positive impact on the work environment you are in. On the other hand, if you are in a more junior role and you see wrong things happening, then, you need to be aware of the right protocol to report them to decision makers, so that they take the right actions. Besides, what's the point of all your knowledge, skills, and expertise if they won't prompt you to make the right choices when the situation calls for it?

The last option if someone retaliates and you reach a dead end, is to consider looking for an alternative, more healthier work environment. The reason why I discuss this concept in chapter 11 of the book is to say; if you closely follow and practice what has been highlighted in the first 10 chapters and become that kind of a profound hotel professional, then you won't be worried about tolerating others wrong doings just to save your job. You would either stay and use your knowledge, skills, and emotional intelligence to deal with such situations, or you will decide to move on to another more exciting challenge, because you are in demand and there is no shortage of opportunities for someone with your capabilities.

O2 *Since we are talking about hospitality and working with people, I'd like to believe that being diplomatic is the best approach to have a successful career, isn't it?*

R2 You need to be mindful of why many people overuse the terms "diplomatic" or "politically correct" to make others feel guilty and get them to do what they want. Here comes the importance of being knowledgeable and having some understanding of human psychology and organizational behavior. People who overstress certain words when an important decision is about to be made are playing mental games. Notice which words are repetitively used by your manager, colleagues or is deeply entrenched in your company culture. At times, this technique is used to encourage positive behavior like the practice of organizational Core Values, Hallmarks, and Guiding Principles. At other times, people use this method to emotionally pressurize and compel others to talk, act or behave in a certain way that would eventually serve their agendas.

Being diplomatic doesn't have to contradict with you being assertive when you need to. Again, it's not either/or. You can still act diplomatically with people and have win-win outcomes. The issue is when you mix up "diplomacy" with "hypocrisy" and think that you are doing great. There is nothing more foolish than deceiving yourself. Think of this, for those people who try to wear masks, flip the truth, and play unethical games to harm others; are they at peace? Do you think they have successful careers? What is their reputation? Are they credible? How long will their careers last at the most? What have they gained in comparison to what they have lost?

You will clearly realize the meaning of being diplomatic when you contemplate the answers to those questions.

Q3 *Isn't there an ideal formula for avoiding conflict in the workplace to minimize operational disturbance and promote better team collaboration?*

R3 Let me first clarify that even though the word "conflict" has a negative connotation, it is actually a healthy thing. It's through conflict we allow ourselves and others to stay true to what's important to us and them. In addition, conflict reveals to us that a problem exists and encourages us to navigate better and more creative solutions. Furthermore, conflict enables us to challenge old assumptions which would likely lead to revising outdated practices and processes. Coming up with new solutions as a result of conflict, would certainly minimize operational disturbance and promote team growth, learning and collaboration. Therefore, at times, conflict must be encouraged not avoided. As Margret Heffernan said: "*When we dare to break the silence, or when we dare to see, and we create a conflict, we enable ourselves and the people around us to do our very best thinking.*"

Not to forget that conflict is especially inevitable in a dynamic sector like travel, tourism, and hospitality, where you serve different stakeholders i.e. employees, customers, suppliers, government, investors, and owners, who hold conflicting interests, yet, you must agree that they will all benefit if the company grows and expands, and this is ultimately the objective of most businesses.

In fact, it's highly commendable how this works in the UAE and specifically in Dubai; where people coming from different cultures and backgrounds and adopting various religious, political, and ideological beliefs and having distinct personal priorities, still work together to achieve common organizational goals regardless of any differences.

Overall, from the endless work and personal experiences I have had so far in my life, I found speaking up more rewarding and liberating in terms of building my self-assurance, gaining respect and credibility and has helped in taking my professional life to higher levels of success and achievements. I believe this is all because I chose to stay true to my values and was also willing to help people around me do their best by not opting for easy decisions all the time but rationalizing and debating the best decision.

Following, are three ways that will help you build your assertiveness and appetite for supporting what's right rather than what's easy:

1. Trust your first instincts. If something doesn't look or feel right in the first instance, chances are it's not. Do what it takes to make it right.

You will come across such situations a lot in your working life. Go back and read chapter 2 (Trust Your Intuition) if you need a refresher. If you have an uncomfortable feeling about a decision that is being made or a specific person, don't try to ignore this feeling or pretend it's not there. Talk to someone you trust about it and see their point of view about the matter. If you need to disconnect and go away to re-evaluate the situation and do some planning in a fresh surrounding, do so. If you still try to work through a situation or with a specific person regardless of your uneasiness, and things progress in a positive direction, then well and good. On the contrary, if it feels like hitting the wall, then stop, make a decision and involve the people concerned to execute your decision. Stay faithful, patient, and strategic during the execution process, as it might take a longer time and things may not always go as planned. You will ultimately get what you want if you persevere.

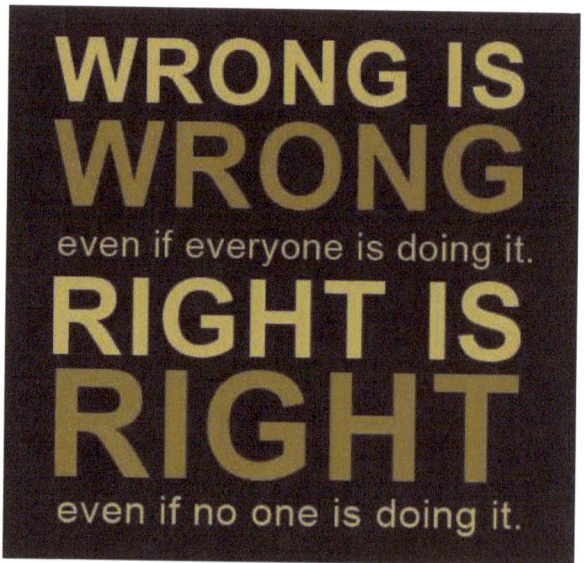

During one of my previous jobs, I had the experience of dealing with an extremely mischievous co-worker. I was getting constant alarms from within to be careful of my interactions with this person, and since I'm someone who doesn't take my intuition for granted, I took note of those feelings and tried to manage the situation in the best possible way. The more I tried to work with this person and overlook her flaws, the more brutal she became in her behavior. I even spoke to her on several occasions about my expectations, but she still didn't make any efforts to improve. The matter reached a very serious point when members of the upper management in the organization started backing her up, regardless of all the facts about her deteriorating performance and attitude that were affecting the department operations and the morale of the rest of employees. At that point, it was very apparent that I was dealing with an ethical dilemma and it was time to put an end to it. Ultimately, I decided to follow company's policies and procedures and terminate her employment because it's the right thing to do. Of course, some people were not very happy about this decision, however, I was confident that this was the best decision for the entire organization, and it turned to be so eventually.

2. Have a balanced approach when dealing with conflict.

Always avoid extremes; aiming for one of the extremes usually makes it difficult for you and the others to move on. Try to sense if others are putting sincere efforts to solve the problem in hand without jeopardizing the relationship, and also be willing to negotiate. Of course, it's not always possible to assess a situation chiefly through vibes and sensations, but as long as you are confident that you did your best to get a win-win outcome, you are fine.

Also remember to re-define your intention at the beginning of every interaction you have with people. Keep your ego out of the room, be humble yet wise. Fulfilment at work doesn't come by winning popularity contests or putting others down; it comes by maintaining your self-respect while gaining the admiration of your colleagues because you are able to lead people and elevate your company's value by knowing how to use your voice.

There were many occasions along my career path where I tried to resolve matters peacefully at first. There were even instances when I felt some of my co-workers were trying to elevate themselves by putting others down. I don't entertain manipulative people anyways and can easily ignore brutal remarks and unkind emails. However, I also know that there are occasions where staying quiet will do more harm than good and the ability to identify those occurrences has come to me from experience.

3. Don't avoid conflict, use it to your advantage.

Prior to reading this chapter, you probably used to feel a bit anxious whenever you heard the word "conflict." That's natural, when you are constantly focused on the negative aspects of something, you will tend to avoid it at any cost. However, this won't be the case for you anymore. If you are serious about your professional growth and reputation, then you need to start identifying suitable opportunities where you can voice your opinion or provide input and do so within the scope of your role and expertise. As you continue doing more and more of this, people will start noticing you and appreciating your contributions and honesty. They will soon start counting on you to speak in situations where they know others won't and you will be a source of inspiration for them.

Workplace Conflicts and Disagreements

People always look up to leaders for inspiration. Leaders are people who do things differently and win the trust of others. As Stephen M. R. Covey mentioned in his bestselling book "The Speed of Trust": trust or credibility is acquired when you have character and competence combined. In my view, the best way to show whether you are a trustworthy person, is when you gather your courage to speak up in times of moral violations, while others choose to stay quiet.

3 Actions you should take as a result of reading this chapter:

1. Familiarize yourself with some of the common behavioral and personality tools like MBTI, DISC and the 4 Color Personality tests. These assessments can provide some insights about various work-related aspects such as personal preferences in communication, decision making, leadership style, etc. which can help promote better understanding for oneself and others in the workplace.

2. Reflect on two previous instances at work, the first one, when you decided to keep quiet despite the strong urge you had to speak up. How did you feel about yourself later? Was it a good decision to keep quiet? What did you learn from that experience? Now think about another scenario, something was going on in front of you, and you couldn't help but express how you felt about the situation. What were you proud about then? Was it a good decision to speak up? What was your learning out of that incident?

3. Learn some techniques that will help you deal with conflict in the workplace effectively. Some of these methods include but is not limited to staying calm, active listening, finding common ground, stating facts, asking the right questions, and picking your battles wisely.

Suggested reading for this chapter:

Are you lacking the tools or skills to manage conflict or discuss a high-stakes matter? If yes, then I recommend that you get the paper or the audio book of "Crucial Conversations" ... I've personally benefited a lot from the tools and stories highlighted throughout this book in my personal and professional life.

"Do what is right, not what is easy nor what is popular."

~ Roy T. Bennett

12
Pay It Forward

"The meaning of life is to find your gift. The purpose of life is to give it away."
~ Anonymous

Life is a continuous cycle of giving and receiving and the most happy and successful people are those who maintain a healthy balance between both ends. The concept discussed in this chapter is quite general and represents the ultimate goal of learning and practicing all the principles discussed in preceding chapters. It's definitely a rewarding act to give, but it's more rewarding to give high-quality knowledge that people are in desperate need of, to help them lead better lives and become more effective in what they do. This is how giving back can benefit you in different ways:

1. Increase Your Joy and Happiness...

There is something magical about giving. Regardless of what you give, many studies have shown that giving to others is the most self-fulfilling act and results in long-lasting internal joy and happiness. We make a living by doing things for ourselves, but we make a life by doing things for others. We all begin our lives aspiring to achieve certain dreams and therefore chase certain goals, which I believe is a good start; nonetheless, along the way, we shouldn't forget to keep contributing within our capacity to find ongoing meaning and happiness in all that we do. As, Mahatma Gandhi said: "*To find yourself, lose yourself in the service of others.*"

2. Be Part of Something Bigger...

It's common to do things for ourselves, and that's ok since it's human nature. We always hear that you can't give what you don't have, however, I believe, at any given time, we always have something or another that we can give, even if it's a genuine smile to make someone's day better or words of hope that help others to push through challenging moments in their life.

You just need to realize that we are all in this planet to fulfil a bigger purpose. Each of us has a piece of the jigsaw puzzle and need to first dig it out and polish it, then put it forth and contribute to assembling the full picture, thus inspiring others to do theirs and contribute in the same way. So, by giving we promote social collaborations and communal partnership and share our gifts with each other. Together we do it better.

3. Allow You to Receive...

What you receive in this world, is a direct by-product of the quality and quantity of what you give to others. I strongly believe that your contributions to this world and how you make other people's life easier as a result of your behaviors, actions and sometimes merely presence, determines what you get in return and become in life. As Jim Rohn said: "*Giving is better than receiving because giving starts the receiving process.*"

Being humans, we at times lose patience and forget that great things in life take time to manifest. We want to see the fruits of our hard work immediately. The secret is to do your part with good intentions and trust God's plan for you. Opportunities will start presenting themselves to you in the right form at the right time if you do your part.

4. Multiply Your Gifts...

In my experience, something amazing happens when you decide to share your knowledge, skills, and talents to make others' lives easier. It's all about having the right intentions, then supplementing them with efforts in the right direction. The more people's lives you impact positively, the more blessings God will shower in your life and He will magnify your results. He will clear your path from all people and events that will impede your progress, and even if they come around they won't be able to harm you. In fact, you can see your knowledge, wisdom and talents being honed and your outcomes being multiplied day in and day out. In summary, good deeds lead to goodwill which create greater possibilities of receiving good news!

5. Stay Composed and Aligned...

Practicing spiritual concepts like giving, collaboration, integrity etc. in your daily life helps you stay aligned. Most people suffer because they constantly live in an internal state of dilemma between what's right and what's easy.

Integrating such values or spiritual beliefs especially in your work life enhances your character, gives you more satisfaction and builds your credibility. We see such values repeated regularly in the corporate world and form an underlying part of many organizations' culture; still, there are very few people around us who believe in making moral values part of their work lives and practicing them, because of their distorted beliefs about reality or lack of understanding of the universal laws. What you put in, you get out and if you focus on the right things, you will always get the right results, and vice versa even if it takes a long time.

★★★

A few years back, I heard an interesting piece of information that startled me. This is in context of the importance of sharing information and giving knowledge. I learned that the more knowledge you acquire, then do nothing with, in terms of either putting it into practice or turning it to meaningful work that will benefit other people; this untapped accumulated knowledge will transform into an inner energy that can cause you more harm than good. This energy can turn into any type of physical or emotional disease that will keep on eating up your inner peace until you decide to share that knowledge to benefit others. I can here recall several examples in my own life when I acquired new knowledge and didn't necessarily spread that. The initial feeling of pride of being well-informed turned into anxiousness that started disturbing my inner peace. Comparatively, whenever I shared my knowledge and expertise (which I've started doing consistently in the past few 3 – 4 years), whether by training people, coaching them or by writing; I have experienced a lot of blessings pouring into my life and I became closer and trusted by people. Realizing and implementing this principle has turned my life around and given me exceptional outcomes in my life.

I reckon, this example is not limited to knowledge but to anything God has given you, which you choose to keep to yourself including all material and non-material aspects of this world. So, the next time you feel a sense of discomfort within you, realize that you need to give out something you have i.e. knowledge, care, time, money, etc. to someone else to gain back your comfort.

People generally gravitate towards those who are generous and giving. It's from the justice of God that he has granted all of us the ability to give something or another and it's

Environmental Initiative Part of Hyatt Thrive by Grand Hyatt Hotel Team in 2013

our role to discover what our special talent is. We then need to invest our time and efforts to grow and develop this talent to help ourselves and others around us. Just imagine spending all your professional life pushing against the wall and not getting anywhere. This is especially true in service based domains like tourism and hospitality.

I find it pointless to spend years of your life working in a sector like hospitality and still operating as a robot who is merely there to do the tasks instead of using your work experience to enhance your skills, expand your network and allow yourself, the people around you, and the industry to enjoy the rewards of this meaningful work. You may need to rethink the way you view and do your work as a hotelier and make necessary changes that will serve you better today and make you proud tomorrow.

Giving is the ultimate purpose to live a fulfilling life. It becomes a really worthwhile experience when you exert your God-given talents, knowledge, and experiences in service of others and practice individual as well as organizational stewardship. You can give in different forms, however, in my humble opinion, the best form of giving should have long-term impact on the receiver, like to give others hope, foundation or solutions that will make their lives easier. Similarly, the main motivation for me to write this book and share it with you is to create hope that nothing is impossible, to show how your daily choices will eventually end up shaping your life and mapping your destiny, and to give you tried and tested solutions on how you can accelerate your hospitality career success by learning and applying the concepts highlighted in this book. As Maimonides said: "*Give a man a fish and you feed him for a day; teach a man how to fish and you feed him for a lifetime.*"

Now, let's tackle some questions that I heard from my colleagues and other professionals about giving:

Q1 *What if I've been constantly putting extra time and efforts in my work, but I feel that I'm still not receiving what I deserve?*

R1 This is a common question that I've been hearing for a while and would like to shed some light on. Throughout my career, I've seen many people working on autopilot and doing things just to tick a box. If most of these people are having this kind of attitude towards their work and not pausing to question themselves "why I'm doing it this way" or "how I can do it better"; then I really believe that such people are truly receiving their fair share of rewards and shouldn't complain at all.

UAE National Day 2013 Celebrations in Grand Hyatt Dubai

In work context, there is an employment contract that determines the rights and responsibilities and governs the relationship between employees and employers. However, anything beyond that will be decided based on the time, efforts, and passion both parties invest in this relationship. For you as an employee, be certain that your employer won't simply give you a pay raise or grant you your next promotion if you just keep on doing the same repetitive work every day for the next 5 or 10 years. You've got to do something unique, valuable, and extra to impress your employer and deserve to get better things in life. This really goes back to the principle that you need to be willing to constantly give with love to activate the process of receiving in your life.

Q2 *What are some forms of giving through which I can pay it forward?*

R2 I personally believe that you can give back something or another in each phase of your life. Paying something forward precisely means that similar to how you've come across people in your life journey who were kind enough to uplift you through their advice, help or support, you need to do the same and help others in some way to continue the chain of good deeds performed by strangers. This will contribute towards making our world a good place to be in. So, as you grow in knowledge, position, and status, you will be able to make a greater impact on your organization and society simply by understanding that there are no limits to how you can help others.

Talking to the HCT Dubai Women's College Students About Career Opportunities in Hospitality During Employer's Forum 2013

If you've gained some useful knowledge, pass it on to others if you know it will help them; if you hold an authoritative position in your organization, use it to reinforce integrity and discourage corruption, and if you have achieved an influential status, then you may want to use it to back up and endorse someone with potential talent in your community to help them progress in their careers. These are some common forms of giving that you may consider during your tenure in the hotel industry, the better you understand your capacity to give, the more effective and credible you will become in what you do.

O3 *What can I do to apply the "Pay It Forward" principle in my career?*

R3 Since the nature of work in hotels involves working with different people, your success and reputation as a hotelier will be highly determined by how moral you are when you deal with those people. Be true to yourself. Don't have dual personalities and double standards, and if you do so, you are fooling no one but yourself. Take advice from people who have the right character as well as expertise. Don't complain about the problems that you have brought onto yourself and take responsibility to figure them out. Stop being passive about your circumstances; blaming others will only make your situation worse and make you less effective. If you don't like how things are in your life, change them, you are not a tree. Know that you have both the choice and the control over your actions and that eventually you will reap only what you sow.

And now, let's learn how to activate the characteristics of giving in our day to day work life that will contribute to your personal and professional effectiveness:

1. Discover your golden coins and polish them.

Every one of us has been given a gift. Our gifts are our innate strengths and talents that we need to identify. You may use one of the several tools mentioned in the previous chapters to do so. The earlier you can identify your God given gifts, the sooner you will be able to determine your life direction and set your plan. Your life plan then needs to highlight the knowledge, skill set, work experiences, relationships, and other aspects that you need to harness your inner gifts and turn them to talents. Of course, you will need to work on yourself first to be able to deliver high quality results depending on which stage of the cycle you are at (mentioned in chapter 7). By doing that, you are focusing your efforts in the right direction and will keep going on regardless of the difficulties. The more value you provide to your colleagues, employer, community, etc., the greater opportunities you will get to cash your golden coins. In other words, your polished talents and unique experiences are your golden coins that you can turn into cash once people around you see the value addition you are bringing to the game.

Life is quite simple, you get out what you put in, and in order to put in high-quality work, you need to first discover your natural talents, make them perfect, then put them in service of other people.

During Colleague of The Month Awards 2006 in Burj Al Arab Jumeirah

I'd like to share with you the driving force that motivated me to pursue my Post Graduate education. I was very fortunate to get my first job opportunity in the Training department of Burj Al Arab Jumeirah. In my capacity there, I used to deliver guest services modules to line colleagues. After 2 years of running training sessions and interacting with most colleagues, I realized that people had started looking up to me and asking me for guidance. This made me very glad to be of help to my colleagues; concurrently, I felt a strong sense of responsibility towards those people who trusted me and my advice. I thought to myself, how can I give them more useful information? What will enable me to stay up to date with all these business-related concepts and practices? How can I polish what I know even more and make it more valuable to my audience? After giving this a deep thought, I decided to leave my hospitality career for a few years to pursue higher education. I used that period to kick off my educational and self-learning journey which is still going on till now. I wanted to know more regarding what I was talking about, so that the people I serve get the best quality knowledge.

I completed my dual MBA in Human Resources Management and Operations Management and supplemented this with a series of internationally recognized certifications in Management & Leadership, Computer Literacy, Training, Quality & Project Management, Human Resources and Coaching. I worked very hard to prepare for those exams and submit those assignments while managing my full-time job. It was neither easy nor rosy but was definitely worth it. I got a great opportunity to get back to hospitality in 2012 with Hyatt Hotels, just three months after I completed my Dual-MBA. I was ready to apply what I'd learnt, and serve people using the knowledge I'd gained, so the opportunity had presented itself to me in the most unexpected way and the rest is history!

2. Turn your challenges into opportunities for creating solutions. Try and test the effectiveness of those solutions, then share them with others who are facing similar circumstances to make their life easier.

Have you ever thought what is the main objective of undergoing challenges in life? There is no doubt that at times, they get very complicated and may slow down our progress, however, these are usually temporary situations to reveal us to ourselves and test our faith and resilience. You have surely experienced many difficult scenarios in your personal and professional life, which you eventually overcame. In that process, you became stronger, wiser, and more experienced in dealing with people and evaluating situations. These have suddenly turned from adversities to a field of opportunities, where you have found solutions to some complicated matters in life, which now can be shared with other people for their benefit. This is the bigger picture and how exactly you should think when you come across one of those harsh moments in life.

In this book, I've talked about some scenarios that if you are not aware of would slow down your career progress and have included suggestions on how to deal with them. It's in my DNA to always make the most of my experiences and be fascinated about what the future can bring, rather than focusing on the current obstacles; you guessed it right, I'm futuristic.

As the situations you encounter in your life are unique to you, the solutions will have to be specific to those issues too. I agree that there will be some common themes and patterns that can be identifiable with other people, but the dimensions will never be all the same, and that's exactly what makes personal stories worth hearing and learning

Featured in The National Newspaper 2016 - A Day In A Life of A Professional

Being someone who chose a new career path among my peers, I've acquired most of my learnings and experiences on how to make a career in hospitality a worthwhile one through trial and error. One example on that is, in my early hotel career, I was working very hard and therefore, managed to get some applauses along the way during my entry level positions. However, as I grew through the ranks, for various reasons, this recognition was diminishing and at times was not there at all. Initially, when I knew that I'd been delivering a series of outstanding work performances but still no one had bothered to appreciate my efforts even verbally, I used to feel agitated. However, with time and experience, I figured out a far better way to receive the recognition I deserve, and this is all through participating in and winning industry awards (as detailed in chapter 10). I learnt how to turn the challenge into an opportunity to shine, get noticed and further recommend this solution to my industry peers who are dealing with similar concerns. The bottom line; use adversities to create opportunities for yourself and others, and this is a remarkable way to pay it forward.

3. Preserve your life experiences and stories in a book, series of books or other published mediums to leave a legacy.

There are various ways to pass on your valuable knowledge and experiences to other people, so they can benefit from it too. You may start with discussion forums, short articles, and blogs, that will ultimately pave the way for you to write your first book and become a published author.

The work of your entire life is purely for you, until you decide to present it in a polished way to the world in a form that others can use and learn from, like books, talks, seminars, webinars, etc. The key intent is to document the events of your life and make them readily available to others to serve their learning and growth. Remember, the more lives you positively touch, the greater will be your blessings.

The Start of My Authoring Journey with Natasa Denman

I decided to write this book to share key aspects of my rich hospitality career, mind you, that's only one aspect of my life. Like most of you, I have learned important lessons in every area of my life and consider those lessons as valuable intellectual assets. Who knows, in the future, I may decide to write about lessons learned relating to money, relationships, or spirituality or start a podcast to discuss my key life learnings in detail. I encourage you to do the same!

3 Actions you should take as a result of reading this chapter:

1. Begin giving on a smaller scale if you are not doing it already. Remember to have the right intentions first to experience the benefits of giving on yourself and others. Giving to tick a box is not giving, it's a task done. Decide "Why" and "What" you are giving and the "How" will present itself to you as a challenge or an opportunity.

2. Identify at least two challenges you are currently facing in your career. Brainstorm possible solutions for each one and draw up an action plan for execution. Foresee yourself after five years from now talking about these challenges to your future team and taking pride in how you introduced effective solutions that now they can use if faced with similar challenges.

3. Think of at least two ways through which you will start imparting your accumulated knowledge and valuable experiences to others to help them learn and progress in their lives. Will you blog, write articles, or start journaling in an attempt to turn that to a published book, a few years from now?

Suggested reading for this chapter:

In his best-selling book "Become A Better You," Joel Osteen offers seven simple yet profound steps to help you discover your purpose and destiny. Joel has helped many people to look within themselves and find their authentic soul and live to their fullest potential. This book will help you learn to enjoy every day of your life, no matter what your circumstances.

"Helping others in need is not only a responsibility of life, it's what gives meaning to life."

~ Mollie Marti

About the Author

Mona AlHebsi, is an award-winning Emirati leader, accomplished hotelier, seasoned HR professional, success coach, and a passionate writer in the field of HR, Hospitality and Leadership. Mona hails from the magnificent mountainous area of Ras Al Khaimah; one of the seven cities in the United Arab Emirates. She was born to a traditional Emirati family and is the eldest of seven siblings. Mona has grown up and completed her schooling in her home town and received her pre-graduate in E-Commerce from The Higher Colleges of Technology, RAK Women's College in 2004. Mona believes in lifelong learning and this is evident in the several academic degrees and professional qualifications that she has been acquiring along the way, which she believes is the key contributing factor to her career success today.

Mona is known to be amongst the very few UAE National women who have pioneered in the hospitality industry since 2005, which was quite an unpopular career choice for Emiratis due to the perceived cultural and societal reservations about the industry. Her first assignment with the iconic "Burj Al Arab" Jumeirah hotel was a fascinating learning experience and her door to a world of glamour, endless discoveries and astounding challenges which made her a well-known hotelier in the MENA region, and an inspiring success story to many of her peers in the industry, especially UAE Nationals.

After more than 13 years of experience in hospitality, education and coaching combined; Mona has decided to share her tried and tested secrets with all working professionals, especially hoteliers; to help them replicate the same outcome in their careers. These exclusive methods, if applied, can make all the difference between "Feeling Stuck" in your job or "Being the Star." Working in hotels is one of the most exciting and fulfilling careers, yet, it can easily be misinterpreted by hoteliers themselves before the wider community. In this book, Mona aspires to reveal to her industry peers that a career in hospitality is what they are willing to make out of it, and has nothing to do with the management, the market or the state of the economy.

The world of work is constantly changing, and thus, the secret to excellence is to think "out of the box," so you can be ahead of the game. Consider yourself a consultant and a brand ambassador for your company rather than just an employee.

For appearances, book signings and speaking engagements, please contact Mona AlHebsi at info@monaalhebsi.com or visit http://www.monaalhebsi.com

Reading Recommendations

The Books that Have Highly Enlightened Me...

1. **Nice Girls Don't Get the Corner Office:** Unconscious Mistakes Women Make That Sabotage Their Careers (A NICE GIRLS Book) - Lois P. Frankel

2. **Lean In:** Women, Work, and the Will to Lead - Sheryl Sandberg

3. **The SPEED of TRUST:** The One Thing That Changes Everything - Stephen M.R. Covey

4. **Crucial Conversations:** Tools for Talking When Stakes Are High, Second Edition - Kerry Patterson, Joseph Grenny, Ron McMillan and Al Switzler

5. **The 7 Habits of Highly Effective People:** Powerful Lessons in Personal Change - Stephen R. Covey

6. **Rich Dad Poor Dad:** What the Rich Teach Their Kids About Money That the Poor and Middle Class Do Not! - Robert T. Kiyosaki

7. **The Total Money Makeover:** A Proven Plan for Financial Fitness - Dave Ramsey

8. **Accelerated Learning Techniques:** The Express Track to Super Intelligence - Brian Tracy and Colin Rose

9. **God Is My CEO:** Following God's Principles in a Bottom-Line World - Larry Julian

10. **The Luck Factor:** The Scientific Study of the Luck Mind - Richard Wiseman

11. **Failing Forward:** Failing Forward: Turning Mistakes Into Stepping Stones for Success – John C. Maxwell

12. **The Road Less Traveled, Timeless Edition:** A New Psychology of Love, Traditional Values and Spiritual Growth - M. Scott Peck

13. **Talk Like TED:** The 9 Public-Speaking Secrets of the World's Top Minds - Carmine Gallo

14. **Start with Why:** How Great Leaders Inspire Everyone to Take Action - Simon Sinek

15. **The Art of Non-Conformity:** Set Your Own Rules, Live the Life You Want, and Change the World - Chris Guillebeau

16. **The Road to Recognition:** The A-to-Z Guide to Personal Branding for Accelerating Your Professional Success in The Age of Digital Media – Seth Price and Barry Feldman

17. **Co-Active Coaching:** Changing Business, Transforming Lives - Henry Kimsey-House, Karen Kimsey-House, Phillip Sandahl and Laura Whitworth

18. **Become a Better You:** 7 Keys to Improving Your Life Every Day - Joel Osteen

19. **Emotional Intelligence:** Why It Can Matter More Than IQ – Daniel Goleman

20. **As a Man Thinketh** - James Allen

Reader's Notes

Reader's Notes

Reader's Notes

Reader's Notes

Reader's Notes

www.ingramcontent.com/pod-product-compliance
Lightning Source LLC
Chambersburg PA
CBHW042049290426
44110CB00001B/2